Tukaram was born in 1608. A the devastating famine of 16 him introspective and religio in his dream by the poet-sain and Lord Vithal who commanded him to write. For a low-caste Shudra to write poetry on religious themes was an encroachment on what the Brahmins considered their reserve. Legend has it that he was driven to drown all his manuscripts in the Indrayani river at Dehu, his native village. Thereafter, it is believed, a fast-unto-death resulted in the reappearance of his manuscripts which had, miraculously, remained intact. Tukaram disappeared at the age of forty-one, leaving behind nearly 5000 poems.

*

Dilip Chitre was born in 1938 in Baroda, India. Among his published works are two collections of Marathi poems—*Kavita* and *Kavitenantarchya Kavita*—a collection of short stories and an anthology of contemporary Marathi poetry in translation. He is also a painter and a film-maker. His feature film *Godam* won the Jury's Special Prize at the Festival des Trois Continents, Nantes, France.

Dilip Chitre lives in Pune with his family.

ACKNOWLEDGEMENTS

Earlier versions of some of the translations in the present selection were published in: *Fakir*, The Ezra-Fakir Press, Bombay; *Delos*, University of Texas, Austin, Texas, USA; *Modern Poetry in Translation*, London, UK; *Translation*, Columbia University School of the Arts, New York, NY, USA; *South-Asian Digest of Literature*, South-Asia Institute, University of Heidelberg, Germany.

Says Tuka was originally commissioned by Adil Jussawala for the XAL-PRAXIS Foundation, Bombay.

Parts of the introduction are based on the Ajneya Memorial Lecture which I delivered under the auspices of the South-Asia Institute of the University of Heidelberg on November 7, 1988. Personal gratitude owed to friends and benefactors, particularly to those who supported me morally and financially in lean periods throughout the last thirty-two years, cannot be explicitly mentioned: it has been like one grand and continuous grant that has made this work possible.

—Dilip Chitre

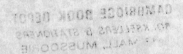

SAYS TUKA
Selected Poetry of Tukaram

*Translated from the Marathi
with an Introduction
by*

Dilip Chitre

PENGUIN BOOKS

Penguin Books India (P) Ltd., B4/246, Safdarjung Enclave,
New Delhi 110 029, India
Penguin Books Ltd., Harmondsworth, Middlesex, England
Penguin Books USA Inc., 375 Hudson Street, New York,
N.Y.10014 USA
Penguin Books Australia Ltd., Ringwood, Victoria, Australia
Penguin Books Canada Ltd., 10 Alcorn Avenue, Suite 300, Toronto,
Ontario M4V 3B2, Canada
Penguin Books (NZ) Ltd. 182-190 Wairau Road, Auckland 10, New Zealand

This translation first published in English by Penguin Books India 1991

Says Tuka *was originally commissioned by Adil Jussawala for the XAL-PRAXIS Foundation, Bombay.*

Typeset in Times Roman by dTech, New Delhi
Made and printed in India by Ananda Offset Private Ltd, Calcutta

*I dedicate this work to all those individuals who believe in keeping poets
(including translators) and poetry alive under the most trying and often
bizarre circumstances that they are perennially susceptible to.*

CONTENTS

Words are the only
Jewels I possess
Words are the only
Clothes I wear
Words are the only food
That sustains my life
Words are the only wealth
I distribute among people

Says Tuka
Witness the Word
He is God
I worship Him
With words

INTRODUCTION

Tukaram was born in 1608 and vanished without a trace in 1649. What little we know of his life is a reconstruction from his own autobiographical poems, the contemporary poetess Bahinabai's memoirs in verse, and the later biographer of Marathi poet-saints, Mahipati's account. The rest is all folklore, though it cannot be dismissed on those grounds alone. Modern scholars such as the late V. S. Bendre have made arduous efforts to collate evidence from disparate contemporary sources to establish a well-researched biography of Tukaram. But even this is largely conjectural.

There is a similar mystery about Tukaram's manuscripts. The Vithoba temple in Tukaram's native village, Dehu, has a manuscript on display that is claimed to be in Tukaram's own handwriting. What is more important is the claim that this manuscript is part of the collection Tukaram was forced to sink in the local river and which was miraculously restored after he undertook a fast-unto-death. The present manuscript is in a somewhat precarious condition and contains only about 250 poems. At the beginning of this century, the same manuscript was recorded as having about 700 poems and a copy of it is still found in Pandharpur. Obviously, the present manuscript has been vandalized in recent times, presumably by scholars who borrowed it from unsuspecting trustees of the temple. It is important to stress that the claim that this manuscript is in Tukaram's own handwriting is not seriously disputed. It is an heirloom handed down to Tukaram's present descendants by their forefathers.

Tukaram had many contemporary followers. According to the *Varkari* pilgrims' tradition, fourteen accompanists supported Tukaram whenever he sang in public. Manuscripts attributed to some of these are among the chief sources from which the present editions of Tukaram's collected poetry derive. Some scholars believe Tukaram's available work to be in the region of about 8000 poems. This is a subject still open to research. The standard edition of the collected poetry of Tukaram is still the one "printed and published under the patronage of the Bombay Government by the proprietors of the Indu-Prakash Press" in 1873. This was reprinted with a new critical introduction in 1950 on the occasion of the tri-centennial of Tukaram's departure and has been reprinted at regular intervals ever since by the Government of Maharashtra. This collection contains 4607 poems in a certain numbered sequence.

In sum, the situation is: (i) We do not have a single complete manuscript of the collected poems of Tukaram in the poet's own handwriting; (ii) We have some contemporary versions but they do not mutually tally; (iii) We have many other versions containing variations on the oldest texts and occasionally, poems that are not found elsewhere.

The various available versions of Tukaram's collected poems are transcriptions made from the oral tradition of the *Varkaris* and/or copies made from other copies of the original collection or contemporary "editions" thereof.

This is a tangled issue best left to the experts. The point to be noted is that every existing edition of Tukaram's collected works is by and large a massive jumbled collection of randomly scattered poems of which only a few are in clearly linked sequences and thematic units. There is no chronological sequence among them. Nor, for that matter, is there an attempt to seek thematic coherence beyond the obvious and broad traditional divisions made by each anonymous "editor" of the traditional texts.

One of the obvious reasons why Tukaram's life is shrouded in mystery and why his work has not been preserved in its original form is because he was born a Shudra, at the bottom of the caste hierarchy. In Tukaram's time in Maharashtra, orthodox Brahmins held that members of all *varnas* other than themselves were Shudras. Shivaji established a Maratha kingdom for the first time only after Tukaram's disappearance. It was only after Shivaji's rise that the two-tier caste structure in Maharashtra was modified to accommodate the new class of kings and warrior chieftains as well as the clans from which they came as proper Kshatriyas.

For a Shudra like Tukaram to write poetry on religious themes in colloquial Marathi was a double encroachment on Brahmin monopoly. Brahmins alone were allowed to learn Sanskrit, "the language of the gods" and to read religious scriptures and discourses. Although since the thirteenth century poet-saint Jnanadev, there had been a dissident *Varkari* tradition of using their native Marathi language for religious self-expression, this had always been in the teeth of orthodox opposition. Tukaram's first offence was to write in Marathi. His second, and infinitely worse offence, was that he was born in a caste that had no right to high, Brahminical religion, or for that matter to any opinion on that religion. Tukaram's writing of poetry on religious themes was seen by the Brahmins as an act of heresy and of defiance of the caste system itself.

In his own lifetime, Tukaram had to brave the wrath of orthodox Brahmins. He was eventually forced to throw all his manuscripts into the local Indrayani river at Dehu, his native village, and was presumably told by his mocking detractors that if indeed he were a true devotee of God, then God would restore his sunken notebooks. Tukaram then undertook a fast-unto-death praying to God for the restoration of his work of a lifetime. After thirteen days of fasting,Tukaram's sunken notebooks reappeared from the river. They were undamaged.

This ordeal-by-water and the miraculous restoration of his manuscripts is the pivotal point in Tukaram's career as a poet and a saint. It seems that after this episode his detractors were silenced, at least for some time.

But Tukaram and his miraculously restored manuscript collection both disappeared soon after this. Some modern writers speculate on the possibility that Tukaram could have been murdered and his work was sought to be destroyed. However, Tukaram was phenomenally popular during his own lifetime and was hailed as "Lord Pandurang incarnate" by contemporary devotees like the poetess Bahinabai. Any attack on his person, let alone a successful attempt on his life, would not have escaped the keen and constant attention of his numerous followers. Therefore, such speculations seem wild and sensational.

Shivaji was born nineteen years before the disappearance of Tukaram. The Maratha kingdom was yet to be founded when Tukaram departed from this world. At this juncture, the whole Deccan region was in the throes of a political upheaval. Trampled by rival armies and ravaged by internecine warfare, small farmers in the villages of Maharashtra faced harrowing times.

Around 1629, there was a terrible famine followed by waves of epidemic diseases. Tukaram's first wife, Rakhma, was an asthmatic, and probably also a consumptive woman. Though he had been married to his second wife Jija while Rakhma was alive, Tukaram loved Rakhma very dearly. Rakhma starved to death during the famine while Tukaram watched in helpless horror.

Shivaji was born within a year of the terrible famine that ruined Tukaram's family as it did thousands of others. Even after Shivaji's rise a few years later, things could not have been better for the average farmer in the villages of Maharashtra. Though Shivaji's brief reign was popular by all accounts, he was battling the might of the Mughal military machine, waging a constant guerilla war.

Relative peace and stability returned to Maharashtra only about a century after Tukaram. While it had tenaciously survived the political turmoil surrounding it, the *Varkari* religious movement witnessed a revival only after the situation became more settled. Tukaram's great grandson, Gopalbawa, played an important role in this revival. Otherwise, for four generations, the history of the Tukaram tradition remained obscure even though increasing numbers of people claimed to have become Tukaram's followers.

*

A brief survey of Tukaram's life and his circumstances gives us an idea of the universality of his experience at a this-worldly level which, in his poetry, acquires other-worldly dimensions.

Tukaram was the second son of his parents, Bolhoba Ambile (or Moré) and Kanakai. Bolhoba had inherited the office of the village Mahajan from his forefathers. Mahajans were a reputed family of traders in a village, *kasba* or city appointed to supervise certain classes of traders and collect revenue from them. Tukaram's family owned a comparatively large piece of prime agricultural land on the bank of the river Indrayani in Dehu. Several generations of Tukaram's ancestors had farmed this land and sold its produce as merchant-farmers. Though, technically regarded as Shudras by Brahmins, they were by no means socially or culturally backward. Being traders by profession, they learnt to read and write as well as to maintain accounts of financial transactions. This was presumably the kind of education Tukaram had. The rest was his own learning from whatever sources he had access to. Considering the situation of the small village of Dehu, it is exciting to speculate on the sources of Tukaram's wealth of information and the depth of his learning.

The early death of his parents and the renunciation of worldly life by his elder brother thrust upon Tukaram the role of the head of his extended Hindu family at a fairly young age. As mentioned earlier in another context, Tukaram was marrried a second time as his first wife was chronically ill. He had six children and had to raise a younger brother as well.

Before he was twenty-one, Tukaram had to witness a series of deaths from amongst his loved ones including his mother, his father, his first wife, and children. The famine of 1629, during which he lost his wife, was a devastating experience for Tukaram. The horror of the human condition that Tukaram speaks of comes from this experience. After the famine, Tukaram lost all urge to lead a householder's life. He showed no interest in farming or the family's trade. Presumably the famine, but also some other circumstance of which we have no details, seems to have reduced Tukaram first to penury and then to the final humiliation of bankruptcy. He was unable to repay the debts he had incurred and the village council stripped him of his position as Mahajan and passed strictures against him. He incurred the displeasure of the village Patil (Headman).

Tukaram became totally withdrawn. He started to shun the company of people. He began to sit alone in a corner and brood. Soon, he started going off into the wilderness for long spells. Meanwhile, his wife had to fend for herself and the children as Tukaram paid little attention to his household responsibilities.

The Ambiles (Morés) of Dehu had been devoted *Varkaris* for several generations before Tukaram. Lord Vithoba of Pandharpur was their family deity. There was a shrine of Vitthal built by an ancestor of Tukaram on land owned by the family in Dehu. A series of traumatic events in his personal life not only made Tukaram introspective but also made him turn his attention to the deity in whom his forefathers had placed their unswerving faith. Their ancestral shrine of Vitthal happened to be in a state of disrepair at this time and Tukaram restored this shrine even though his immediate family was reduced to abject misery.

He now began to spend most of his time in the shrine of Vitthal or its precincts, singing songs composed by earlier poet-saints in praise of the deity. He totally disregarded the pleas of his wife and the counsel of his friends and virtually stopped working for a living. He became a drop-out and perhaps an object of pity or contempt among many of his fellow-villagers. His wife and some of his fellow-villagers saw this as a form of madness because Tukaram was lost to the world and had broken away from its routines and practical bonds. However, his total devotion to Vitthal and his compassion for everybody and all forms of life slowly won him the admiration of people.

Some time at this juncture, Tukaram had a revelatory dream in which the great poet-saint Namdeo and Tukaram's deity Vitthal appeared and initiated Tukaram into poetry, informing Tukaram that his mission in life was "to make poems". "Poems" of course meant "*abhangs*" to be sung in praise of Vithoba as Namdeo himself had done. The dream made reference to a pledge made by Namdeo to

Vitthal that he would compose "one billion *abhangs*" in His praise. Namdeo had obviously been unable to achieve this steep target in his lifetime and he therefore asked Tukaram to complete the task. This dream or revelation which he saw while in a state of trance was so vivid that Tukaram was convinced of its "reality". This changed his life. He had found his true vocation.

The divine revelation that he was a poet did not cause Tukaram to go into ecstasy. Instead, he began to suffer from anxiety, doubt, and pangs of conscience. One of Tukaram's characteristics was his absolute honesty and accountability to himself. He would not tell a lie even in a poem. The knowledge that his task in life was to write poems in praise of Vitthal made Tukaram a restless and troubled soul. He had never experienced God. How was he going to praise something that he had not experienced himself? He had been an honest trader. He vouched for the quality of every item he sold. He bought goods only after critically testing them. He did not cheat anyone in any transaction. Nor would he allow himself to be cheated. Tukaram treated poetry as serious business from the outset. To him, all poetry was empirical and so was all religion. Experience or "realization" was the crucial test. In one of his poems, presumably written at this juncture, Tukaram says in effect, "whereof I have no experience, thereof I cannot sing. How can I write of You, O Vitthal, When I have not personally experienced Your being?" Yearning for an experience of God became the chief theme of poetry for Tukaram in his first major phase of work. Meanwhile, he continued to record in his poems the human condition as witnessed by him and also his own experiences just prior to his realization that he was to be a poet of God.

Having become a poet, Tukaram continued to go off for long periods of time, away from the hub of human life and society, to meditate and to seek enlightenment. Two hills in the vicinity of Dehu were his favourite retreats. The first is the Bhandara hill, where, in a small cave which is a relic of Buddhist times, he composed many of his *abhangs*. The second is the Bhamchandra hill, where, some years later, he meditated for a full fifteen days before experiencing mystical illumination and beatitude. This event is distinct from another instance of initiation by a guru during a trance that Tukaram has described elsewhere. In this latter event, Tukaram was dreaming that he was going to a river for a dip when he was suddenly confronted by a holy man who placed his hand on Tukaram's head and gave him the *mantra*, "*Rama Krishna Hari*" to chant. This holy man told Tukaram that his name was "Babaji" and that he was a lineal spiritual descendant of the gurus Raghav Chaitanya and Keshav Chaitanya. When Tukaram was given this *mantra*, he felt his entire being come alive. He experienced a fullness of being he had never before felt.

Tukaram himself has described these experiences in his poems and there is no ambiguity about them. Unfortunately, the chronology of these events is difficult to determine except in a broad way. Tukaram must have been thirty years old or more by the time the latter of these experiences occurred. A prominent modern biographer of Tukaram, the late V.S. Bendre, has laid great emphasis on Tukaram's dream-initiation by "Babaji" and the guru-lineage it signifies. I suspect that *Bhakti* has roots in folk-religion and therefore Brahmin and caste Hindu people always try to "upgrade" a *Bhakta* by presenting him as a "*yogi*" or an "initiate" of some esoteric order or another. Bendre appears to me to have been attempting to "Brahminize" Tukaram through "*yogic*" and "*mantric*" initiation rites performed by a "proper" guru. This seems to be an attempt to authenticate a natural and self-made *Bhakta*. But to me the meaning of these stories is almost the opposite: to a "Shudra" the guru can appear *only* in a "dream" or a trance.

Now the last and the most spectacular decade in Tukaram's life begins. Though Tukaram was only about thirty years old at this time, he had been writing poetry for nearly ten years. In his poetry, Tukaram had depicted with great honesty his own past life and his anguished search for God. With his recent mystical enlightenment, his poetry acquired a magical lyrical quality. His songs began to attract people from distant places. The younger poetess Bahinabai came to Dehu all the way from Kolhapur just to witness Tukaram's divine performance of his poetry in front of the image of Vitthal in the shrine near his ancestral house. Though Bahinabai's account of her visit to Dehu refers to a period just a few years before Tukaram's disappearance, from her description we get some idea of the charismatic influence of Tukaram upon his contemporaries throughout Maharashtra. The water-ordeal that has been referred to earlier had already taken place before Bahinabai's visit to Dehu. The miraculous restoration of his manuscripts that had been consigned to the river for thirteen days was surely a major factor contributing to the legendary status which Tukaram acquired in his lifetime. Bahinabai has described Tukaram singing his *abhangs* as "Lord Pandurang incarnate". "Whatever Tukaram writes is God," says Bahinabai.

Tukaram disappeared at the age of forty-one. *Varkaris* believe that Vitthal Himself carried Tukaram away to heaven in a "chariot of light". Some people believe that Tukaram just vanished into thin air while singing his poetry in front of an ecstatic audience on the bank of the river Indrayani in Dehu. Some others as I have said, speculate that he was murdered by his enemies. Still others think that he ended his own life by throwing himself into the very river where his poems had been sunk earlier. Reading his farewell poems, however, one is inclined to imagine that Tukaram bade a proper farewell to his close friends and fellow-devotees and left his native village for some unknown destination with no intention of returning. He asked them to return home after their having walked a certain distance with him. He told them that they would never see him again as he was "going home for good". He told them that from then on only "talk about Tuka" would remain in "this world".

This, in short, is the story of Tukaram's life as it emerges from his own poems. One can see from it that from absolutely ordinary origins and after having gone through experiences accessible to average human beings anywhere, Tukaram went on an extraordinary voyage of self-discovery while continuing to record every stage of it in detail in his poetry. His poetry is a unique document in human history, impeccably centred in the fundamental problems of being and defining poetry as both the being of language and the language of being: the human truth.

The first, and by far the only complete translation of *Tukaramachi Gatha* or *The Collected Tukaram* into English was done by J. Nelson Fraser and K.B. Marathe. This was published by the Christian Literature Society, Madras (1909–1915). The only other European language version of the selected poems of Tukaram is G.A. Deleury's *Toukaram: Psaumes du perlerin* (Gallimard; Paris, 1956). Fraser and Marathe's translation comprises 3721 poems in all. Justin E. Abbott's monumental 11-volume series, *Poet-Saints of Maharashtra* (Scottish Mission Industries; Poona, 1926) and Nicol Macnicol's *Psalms of Maratha Saints* (Christian Literature Society; Calcutta, 1919) contain much fewer. Fraser and Abbott have both attempted prose paraphrases while Macnicol has superimposed a heavily stylized verse-form quite alien to the fluid colloquial folk-style of the original. Deleury's 101 poems in French translation are the only European attempt to create a poetic analogue of Tukaram's original work. The distinguished Anglo-Marathi poet, Arun Kolatkar has published 9 translations of Tukaram's poems (*Poetry India*; Bombay, 1966) and my own earlier versions of Tukaram have appeared in *Fakir, Delos,*

Modern Poetry in Translation, Translation, and the *South-Asian Digest of Literature*.

This is hardly an adequate bibliography considering Tukaram's towering stature as a poet and his pervasive influence on Marathi language and literature. He represents the vital link in the mutation of a medieval Marathi literary tradition into modern Marathi literature. His poems (nearly 5000) encompass the entire gamut of Marathi culture. The dimensions of his work are so monumental that they will keep many future generations of translators creatively occupied. In a sense, therefore, Tukaram is a poet who belongs more to the future than to a historically bound specific past.

The translators of Tukaram fall into different categories. Fraser and Abbott have rendered Tukaram into prose, rather like representing a spontaneous choreography as a purposeful walk. Macnicol turns the walk into what seems like a military march. Only Deleury and Kolatkar approach it as dance and in the spirit of dance. Deleury dwells on the lyrical nuance and the emotional intensity of the original. Kolatkar concentrates on the dramatic, the quick and the abrupt, the startling and the cryptic element in Tukaram's idiom. This is hardly enough to give an idea of the range, the depth, and the complexity of the source text as a whole. Tukaram forces one to face the fundamental problem of translating poetry: beneath the simple and elegant surface structure of the source text lies a richer and vastly complex deep structure that the target text must somehow suggest. This is nothing short of a project lasting an exasperating lifetime. It is much easier to play-act the role of Tukaram as a stylized vignette in whatever the prevailing *etat de langue* permits. The culture of poetry is more biased and partisan than the culture of translation. One would hesitate to elaborate on this point at this juncture; but it needs to be made, albeit in passing.

Problems of translation can be compared to problems of instrumentation. The naked eye does not see what can be seen only through a telescope; but a radio telescope literally makes the invisible visible. An electron microscope is designed to "see" what lies beyond sight by definition.

Unfortunately, there is no equipment engineered to read beneath the surface structure of a specific source text. If the target text is only an attempt to create a model of the source text, then every aspect of the source text becomes equally sacrosanct and translation becomes obviously impossible.

Unless the translator presumes or directly apprehends how the source text functions, he cannot begin to look for a possible translation. Poems function in delicate, intricate, and dynamic ways. Their original existence does not depend on specific audiences or the possibility of eventual translators. No translation can absolutely do away with the idea of the source text as an autonomously functioning whole in another linguistic space and time.

There is an implicit strangeness in every translated work, especially in translated poetry. A translated poem is, at best, an intimate stranger among its counterparts in the target language. The stranger will retain traces of an odd accent, peculiar turns of phrase, exotic references, and even a wistful homesick look. These are happy signs that poetry is born and is alive and kicking elsewhere, too. That other minds do exist is a fact that should be as often celebrated as it is mourned by some puritanical critics.

Religion in Maharashtra, in Tukaram's time, was a practice that separated communities, classes, and castes. *Bhakti* was the middle way between the extremes of Brahminism on the one hand and folk-religion on the other. It was also the most democratic and egalitarian community of worshippers, sharing a way of life and caring for all life with a deep sense of compassion. The legacy of Jainism and Buddhism had not disappeared altogether in Maharashtra. It was regenerated in the form of *Bhakti*. Tukaram's penetrating criticism of the degenerated state of Brahminical Hinduism, and his scathing comments on bigotry and obscurantism, profiteering and profligacy in the name of religion, bear witness to his universal humanistic concerns. He had the abhorrence of a true realist for any superstitious belief or practice. He understood the nature of language well enough to understand how it can be used to bewitch, mislead, and distort. He had a healthy suspicion of god-men and gurus. He believed that the individual alone was ultimately responsible for his own spiritual liberation. He was not an escapist. His mysticism was not rooted in a rejection of reality but rather in a spirited response to it after its total acceptance as a basic fact of life. Tukaram's hard common sense is not contradicted by his mysticism: the two reinforce each other.

The Marathi poet-saints are an exception to the general rule that Indian devotional literature shows little awareness of the prevailing social conditions. The Marathi "saints", both implicitly and explicitly, questioned the elitist monopoly of spiritual knowledge and privilege embodied in the caste hierarchy. They were strongly egalitarian and preached universal love and compassion. They trusted their native language, Marathi, more than the Sanskrit of the scriptures or the erudite commentaries thereon. They made language a form of shared religion and religion a shared language. It is they who helped to bind the Marathas together against the Mughals on the basis not of any religious ideology but of a territorial cultural identity. Their egalitarian legacy continues into modern times with Jotiba Phule, Vitthal Ramji Shinde, Chattrapati Shahu, Sayaji Rao Gaekwar, and B.R. Ambedkar—all outstanding social reformers and activists. The gamut of *Bhakti* poetry has amazing depth, width, and range : it is hermitic, esoteric, cryptic, mystical; it is sensuous, lyrical, deeply emotional, devotional; it is vivid, graphic, frank, direct; it is ironic, sarcastic, critical; it is colloquial, comic, absurd; it is imaginative, inventive, experimental; it is intense, angry, assertive and full of protest. In the 4000-plus poems of Tukaram handed down to us by an unbroken oral tradition, there are poems to which all the above adjectives fit.

The tradition of the Marathi saints conceives the role of a poet in its own unique way and I am sure this has a deep ethno-poetic significance. *Bhakti* is founded in a spirit of universal fellowship. Its basic principle is sharing. The deity does not represent any sectarian dogma to the *Bhakta* but only a common object of universal love or a common spiritual focus. Poetry is another expression of the same fellowship. Tukaram may have written his poems in loneliness but he recited them to live audiences in a shrine of Vitthal. Hundreds of people gathered there to listen to his poetry. The poetess Bahinabai, a contemporary and a devoted follower of Tukaram, has described how Tukaram, in a state of trance, chanted his poems while an enraptured audience rocked to their rhythm.

This had been a tradition from the time of Jnanadev (1275—1296), the founder of Marathi poetry and the cult of Vithoba and Namdeo (1270–1350), the great forerunner of Tukaram. The audience consisted of common village-folk, including women and low-caste people, thrilled by the heights their own language scaled and stirred by the depths it touched.

Paul Valery defines the difference between prose and poetry as comparable to the difference between walking and dancing: and Tukaram's recitation must have seemed to his audience like pure dance, turning nothingness into space.

Life, in all its aspects was the subject of such poetry. Tukaram himself believed that he was only a medium of the poetry, saying, "God speaks through me." This was said in humility and not with the pompous arrogance of a god-man or the smug egoism of a poet laureate.

The saints are perhaps inaccurately called so because the Marathi word "*sant*" used for them sounds so similar. The Marathi word is derived from the Sanskrit "*sat*" which denotes being and awareness, purity and divine spirit, wisdom and sagacity, the quality of being emancipated, and of being true. The relative emphases are somewhat different in the Christian concept of sainthood, though there is an overlap.

The poet-saint fusion in Marathi gives us a unique view of poetry itself. In this view, moral integrity and spiritual greatness are critical characteristics of both poetry and the poet.

Tukaram saw himself as primarily a poet. He has explicitly written about being a poet, the responsibility of a poet, the difficulties in being a poet and so forth. He has also criticized certain kinds of poetry and poets. It is clear that he would have agreed with Heidegger that in poetry the language of being becomes one with the being of language. Poetry was, for him, a precise description of the human condition in its naked totality. It was certainly not an *effete* form of entertainment for him. Nor was it ornamental. Language was a divine gift and it had to be returned to its source, via poetry, with selfless devotion.

This could sound like a cliche, but Tukaram's genius partly lies in his ability to transform the external world into its spiritual analogue. The whole world became a sort of functional metaphor in his poetry, a text. His poems have an apparently simple surface. But beneath the simple surface lies a complex understructure and the tension between the two is always subtly suggested.

The famous "signature line" of each poem, "Says Tuka" opens the door to the deeper structure. Aphoristic, witty, satirical, ironic, wry, absurd, startling or mystical, these endings of Tukaram's poems often set the entire poem into sudden reverse motion. They point to an invisible, circular or spiral continuity between the apparent and the real, between everyday language and the intricate world-image that it often innocently implies.

Thus, Tukaram sees the relationship between God and His devotee as the relationship between a master and a dog or as that between an adultress and her clandestine or forbidden lover. Tukaram is not proposing the absolutely external existence of God, independent of man. He knows that it is the devotee who creates an anthropomorphic image of God. He knows that in a sense it is a make-believe God entirely at the mercy of his creator-devotee using a man-made language.

Tukaram is interested in a godlike experience of being where there is no boundary between the subjective and the objective, the personal and the impersonal, the individual and the cosmic. He sees his own consciousness as a cosmic event rooted in the everyday world but stretching infinitely to the deceptive limits of awareness. "Too scarce to occupy an atom," he writes, "Tuka is as vast as the sky."

One of the more striking aspects of Tukaram's poetry is its distinct ethno-poetics or the *Marathiness* of its conception.

Medieval Marathi poetry developed in two divergent directions. One continued from the Sanskrit classics—both religious and secular—and from the somewhat different classicism of Prakrit poetry. In either case, it followed older, established models and non-native literary sources. Imitations of Sanskrit models in a highly Sanskritized language and using Sanskrit prosody as well as stylistic devices characterize this trend in Marathi literature. These "classicists" neglected or deliberately excluded the use of native resources of demotic, colloquial Marathi. Luckily, though this trend has continued in Marathi for the last 700 years, only a minority of writers (of not too significant talent) have produced such "classicist" literature.

Others, starting from the pioneer of Marathi *Bhakti* poetry, Jnanadev, took precisely the opposite course. They used the growing resources of vigorously developing Marathi language to create a new literature of their own. They fashioned out a Marathi prosody from the flexible metres of the graceful folk-songs of women at work in homes and of devotees at play in religious folk-festivals. They gave literary form to colloquial speech, drawing their vocabulary from everyday usage of ordinary people. The result was a poetry far richer in body and more variegated in texture than the standardized work of the "classicists". Peopled by many voices, made distinctive by many local and regional tonalities and enriched by spontaneous folk innovation, *Bhakti* poetry became a phenomenal movement bringing Marathi-speaking people together as never before. This poetry was sung and performed by audiences that joined poet-singers in a chorus. Musical-literary discourses or *keertans* that are a blend of oratory, theatre, solo and choral singing and music were the new art-form spawned by this movement. *Bhajan* was the new form of singing poetry together and emphasizing its key elements by turning chosen lines into a refrain. These comprise a new kind of democratic literary transaction in which even illiterates are drawn to the core of a literary text in a collective realization of some poet's work. This open-ended and down-to-earth nativism found its fullest expression in Tukaram, three centuries after Jnanadev and Namdeo had broken new ground by founding demotic Marathi poetry itself.

Bhakti poetry as a whole has so profoundly shaped the very world-image of Marathi speakers that even unsuspecting moderns cannot escape its pervasive mould. But Tukaram gave *Bhakti* itself new existential dimensions. In this he was anticipating the spiritual anguish of modern man two centuries ahead of his time. He was also anticipating a form of personal, confessional poetry that seeks articulate liberation from the deepest traumas man experiences and represses out of fear. Tukaram's poetry expresses pain and bewilderment, fear and anxiety, exasperation and desperateness, boredom and meaninglessness—in fact all the feelings that characterize modern self-awareness. Tukaram's poetry is always apparently easy to understand and simple in its structure. But it has many hidden traps. It has a deadpan irony that is not easy to detect. It has deadly paradoxes and a savage black humour. Tukaram himself is often paradoxical: he is an image-worshipping iconoclast; he is a sensuous ascetic; he is an intense *Bhakta* who would not hesitate to destroy his God out of sheer love. Tukaram knows that he is in charge of his own feelings and the meaning of his poetry. This is not merely the confidence of a master craftsman; it is much more. It is his conviction that man is responsible for his own spiritual destiny as much as he is in charge of his own worldly affairs. He believes that freedom means self-determination. He sees the connection between being and making choices. His belief is a conscious choice for which he has willingly paid a price.

Tukaram is therefore not only the last great *Bhakti* poet in Marathi but he is also the first truly modern Marathi poet in terms of temper and thematic choice, technique and vision. He is certainly the most vital link between medieval and modern Marathi poetry.

Tukaram's stature in Marathi literature is comparable to that of Shakespeare in English or Goethe in German. He could be called the quintessential Marathi poet reflecting the genius of the language as well as its characteristic literary culture. There is no other Marathi writer who has so deeply and widely influenced Marathi literary culture since. Tukaram's poetry has shaped the Marathi language, as it is spoken by 50 million people today and not just the literary language. Perhaps one should compare his influence with that of the King James version of the Bible upon speakers of the English language. For Tukaram's poetry is also used by illiterate millions to voice their prayers or to express their love of God.

Tukaram speaks the Marathi of the common man of rural Maharashtra and not of the elite. His language is not of the Brahmin priests. It is the language of ordinary men such as farmers, traders, craftsmen, labourers and also the language of the average housewife. His idiom and imagery is moulded from the everyday experience of people though it also contains special information and insights from a wide variety of sources and contexts. Tukaram transforms the colloquial into the classic with a universal touch. At once earthy and other-worldly, he is able to create a revealing analogue of spiritual life out of this-worldly language. He is, thus, able to prove how close to common speech the roots of great poetry lie. Yet his poetry does not yield the secret of its seamless excellence to even the most sophisticated stylistic analysis. He is so great an artist that his draughtsmanship seems to be an integral part of a prodigious instinct, a genius.

Tukaram's prolific output, by and large, consists of a single spiritual autobiography revealed in its myriad facets. It defies any classification once it is realized that common thematic strands and recurrent motifs homogenize his work as a whole. In the end what we begin to hear is a single voice—unique and unmistakable—urgent, intense, human and erasing the boundary between the private domain and the public. Tukaram is an accessible poet and yet he is a very difficult one. He keeps growing on you.

I attempted my first translation of a Tukaram *abhang* in 1956 or more than thirty years ago. It was the famous *abhang* describing the image of Vitthal—*sundar te dhyan ubha vitevari*. For some reason, at that time I found it comparable to Rainer Maria Rilke's *Archaic Torso of Apollo* and felt that the difference between Vitthal and Apollo described the difference between two artistic cultures. I was only eighteen then and should therefore be forgiven my immature and rash cross-comparison. But the fact is that the comparison persisted in my mind. Through Rilke's poem I reached back to Nietzsche's brilliant early work, *Birth of Tragedy from the Spirit of Music*. This is where Nietzsche first proposed the opposition between Dionysius and Apollo and the resolution of this opposition in Attic Tragedy. I began to look at the iconography of Vitthal to contemplate its secret meaning for *Varkari Bhakta* poets and it was worth paying attention to the unique stance of Vitthal.

The reason I recall this here is because I kept translating the same *abhang* periodically and my most recent version of it was done last year. Each of these versions derive from and point to the same source text. The same translator has attempted them. But can one say that any one of them is more valid or correct or true than any other? Do these translations exist independently of the source text? Do they exist independently of one another? Or do they belong to a vast and growing body of Tukaram literature that now includes many other things in many languages besides the source text of Tukaram's collected poetry? These issues are fundamental to literary theory and to the theory of literary translation, if such a theory were possible.

In this connection, I would like to quote somewhat extensively from my Ajneya Memorial Lecture delivered at the South Asia Institute of the University of Heidelberg in November 1988. The theme of my lecture was the life of a translator and more specifically my life as a translator of Tukaram into a modern European language. Here are some relevant excerpts:

"Someone has said (and I wish it was me who first said it) that when we deal with the greatest of writers, the proper question to ask is not what we think of them but what they would have thought of us. What a contemporary European reader thinks of Tukaram is thus a less proper question to ask than what Tukaram would have thought of a contemporary European reader. Part of my almost impossible task is to make the reader of my translations aware that my translations faced a challenge I was unable to meet. . . ."

". . .*Bhakti*, the practice of devoted awareness, lies in mirroring God here and now. Tukaram was a *Bhakta*-poet. To understand God's being, to translate His presence, he mirrored Him. First, he thought of God, tried to picture Him in various worldly and other-worldly situations. Then he pined for Him. And finally, "possessed" by Him, He acted, through language, like God. To read Tukaram's poetry is to understand this ritual choreography as a whole; for its form is shaped by its function. Thus, in translating Tukaram, we are not merely transposing poetry but recreating a dramatic ritual of "possessed" language. This is the only aspect of Tukaram's work which is multifaceted. But it is a culture-specific aspect of his idea of the role of poetry in life as *Bhakti*."

"This imposes comprehensive constraints upon any would-be translator of Tukaram into any modern European language. He has to be thoroughly aware of the phenomenon of Tukaram at source, not only the text but the context as well. For the text is a total cultural performance which embodies a specific tradition and an individual notion of poetry, the poet and his audience. When Tukaram claims to be a poet he is also claiming that his kind of utterance is poetry as distinct from other kinds of Marathi utterances. He and his tradition in the seventeenth century are innocent of Europe and its poetry. The source language and its literature, in this case, have no actual historical nexus with the target language. This does not rule out, however, an imaginative manipulation of the resources of the target language and literature, as available in the twentieth century, to put Tukaram's work across. In fact, our contemporary translation of Tukaram must make his work appear here and now, yet suggesting also that it is really out there. The translation must subtly contain its own perspective and imagined laws of projected perception, so that Tukaram remains a seventeenth century Marathi *Bhakta*-poet in English translation, and not a jeans-and-jacket-clad European talking of mystical illumination in India. . . ."

More than three decades of translating Tukaram have helped me to learn to live with problems that can only be understood by people who often live in a no-man's land between two linguistic cultures belonging to two distinct civilizations.

As I have said earlier, traditional editions of Tukaram's collected works have been compiled from later devotees' versions of orally preserved and transmitted verses. Some of them are copies of still older copies but what we have in supposedly Tukaram's own handwriting is the remaining 250 *abhangs* from the hallowed heirloom of a copy in the temple at Dehu. As I have remarked, this manuscript has been gradually depleting. As a result, there is no canonical text of Tukaram's collected works. The nearest thing to an authorized version that we have access to is *Tukarambavachya Abhanganchi Gatha* collated and critically edited by Vishnu Parshuram Shastri Pandit with the assistance of Shankar Pandurang Pandit in 1873. It is significant to note that one of the four manuscripts used by the Pandits for their critically collated edition was the "Dehu manuscript obtained from Tukaram's own family and continuing in it as an heirloom". But according to the editors, "It is said to be in the hand-writing of Mahadevabava, the eldest son of Tukaram, and so appears to be more than two hundred years old." However, the present oldest direct lineal descendent of Tukaram, Mr. Shridharbuva Moré (Dehukar) informs me that the Dehu manuscript is in Tukaram's own handwriting and is referred to as the *"Bhijki Vahi"* or the "Soaked Notebook".

Whether the Dehu manuscript is in Tukaram's own handwriting or not, its antiquity is not in question. Tukaram's descendants have proudly preserved this copy as an heirloom. The three other copies consulted by the Pandits for their critical edition are the Talegava manuscript of Trimbak Kasar, the Pandharpur manuscript, and the Kadusa manuscript of Gangadhar Mavala. Despite the vigilance of the editors, interpolations may have gone unnoticed in this otherwise excellent and most reliable edition. This is the principal source text I have used although I have occasionally used other *Varkari* editors' versions such as Jog's, Sakhare's, and Neoorgaonkar's.

What struck me, as a regular reader of the collected poems of Tukaram in various editions, was not textual variations as such but the widely divergent sequencing of the *abhangs*. Although there are many distinct groups of *abhangs* that are linked by narrative or thematic connections or have subjects and topics that are clearly spelt out, there is no clue to the chronology of Tukaram's works. They appear in a random sequence and are often a rather jumbled collection of poems without individual titles. In short, what the *Gatha* lacks is a coherent order or an editorial plan, whether thematic or chronological. Since the *Gatha* as a whole is largely an autobiographical work occasionally containing narrative poems, topical poems, poems on specific themes, odes, epistolary poetry, aphoristic verses, prayers, poetry using the personae of various characters, allegories and many other types of poetry, it is difficult to understand it in totality.

Yet I, for one, feel compelled to have a holistic grasp of *Tukaramachi Gatha*. Since I perceive it as an autobiography, even if I cannot suggest a chronological order for the more than 4000 poems before me, I should be able to relate a majority of these poems to Tukaram's personality and his concerns, the key events that shaped his life and his development as a spiritual person through the various transformations his poetry goes through. This book makes an effort to understand Tukaram as a whole being with certain characteristic aspects: it is an introduction to Tukaram, the poet, and his poetry as facets of his being. I have made the same attempt in my Marathi book, *Punha Tukaram*, in which I present an identical selection of *abhangs* in the original Marathi of Tukaram with an introduction, a sort of running commentary, and an epilogue. But the Marathi book is addressed to the insider and is meant to be a critique of Marathi culture, among other things. In the present book, my bilingualism functions on an altogether different level though the two aspects are not mutually exclusive. I have tried to introduce my reader in English to the greatest of Marathi poets, assuming that they are unacquainted with works in Marathi. One of the greatest rewards of knowing this language is access to Tukaram's work in the original.

This book has been divided into ten sections : 1. Being A Poet; 2. Being Human; 3. Being A Devotee; 4. Being In Turmoil; 5. Being A Saint; 6. Being A Sage; 7. Being In Time And Place; 8. Being Blessed; 9. Absolutely Being; 10. A Farewell To Being.

These ten aspects or dimensions of Tukaram's personality are integral to his being as a whole. None of them exists to the exclusion of any other. None of them can be emphasized at the expense of another. These aspects cannot be seen in any linear or serial order, whether chronological or psychological. They are perceived distinctly only because most of his personal and autobiographical poetry falls into place if grouped according to these aspects.

Perceived according to this design, Tukaram's aspects are his inner needs as well as his capabilities. They indicate his sensitivity. They point to his ethics. They imply an entire world-view. These ten aspects cover the universe of Tukaram's awareness.

Once I became aware of these ten facets of Tukaram's life and his poetry, the poems in this book selected themselves. If I have left out some very well-known *abhang* from this selection, the reason could be my self-imposed constraints. I have so far finalized the translation of about 600 abhangs of Tukaram. In selecting poems for this book, my guiding principle was the idea of presenting a poetic self-portrait by Tukaram. There are other ways of looking at his work that is oceanic in its immensity and this is only one of many possible beginnings.

Tukaram is part of a great tradition in Marathi literature that started with Jnanadev. Broadly speaking, it is part of the pan-Indian phenomenon of *Bhakti*. In Maharashtra, *Bhakti* took the form of the cult of Vithoba, the Pandharpur-based deity worshipped by *Varkari* pilgrims who make regular journeys to Pandharpur from all over the region. Jnanadev gave the *Varkari* movement its own sacred texts in Marathi in the form of *Jnanadevi* or *Bhavarthadeepika* (now better known as *Jnaneshwari*) *Anubhavamrita* and *Changdev Pasashti*, as well as several lyrical prayers and hymns. His contemporaries included Namdeo, another great Marathi poet and saint, and a whole galaxy of brilliant poets and poetesses. These poet-*Bhaktas* of Vithoba composed and sang songs on their regular trips to Pandharpur and back from all parts of Maharashtra. In the sixteenth century, the

Varkari tradition produced its next great poet, Eknath and he was followed in the seventeenth century by Tukaram.

Tukaram's younger contemporary, Bahinabai Sioorkar, has used the metaphor of a temple to describe the *Varkari* tradition of *Bhakti*. She says that Jnanadev laid its foundation, Namdeo built its walls, Eknath gave it a central pillar, and Tukaram became its "crown" or "spire". As visualized by Bahinabai, the *Varkari* tradition was a single architectural masterpiece produced collectively by these four great poets and their several talented followers. She rightly views it as a collective work of art in which parts created in different centuries by different individuals are integrated into a whole that only the genius of a common tradition could produce.

The achievement of the Marathi *Varkari* poets is paralleled by only one example I can think of and that too, incidentally, is from Maharashtra. The frescoes of Ajanta and the sculptures and architecture of Ellora comprise similar continuous collective work of superbly integrated art. These were produced by a creative culture that does not lay too great a stress on individual authorship. It is a community of the imagination and a synergy of creative inspiration that sustains such work over several generations.

The secret appears to be the ethos of *Bhakti*.

The roots of *Bhakti* lie more in folk-traditions of worship than in classical Hindu philosophy. As for the *Varkaris*, their only philosopher was Jnanadev. Jnanadev was an ordained member of the esoteric Shaivaite *Natha* sect. It was novel, to say the least, for him to embrace the cult of Vithoba and to give it a philosophical basis on the lines of the Kashmir Shaivagama Acharyas' teachings. Jnanadev's mind was as brilliant and original as Abhinavgupta's. In *Anubhavamrita*—his seminal work in religious philosophy—Jnanadev describes *Bhakti* as *chidvilasa* or "the spontaneous play of creative consciousness". Tukaram celebrates the legacy of Jnanadev in his poetic world-view. But Tukaram reaches the ecstatic state of liberated life only after extreme suffering and an anguished search of a lifetime.

No Marathi reader can read Tukaram except in the larger context of the tradition of *Varkari* poetics and practice of poetry. If readers of Tukaram in translation find him rewarding then they should go deeper into the *Varkari* poetic tradition. They will not be disappointed. They will even discover richer resonances in the same work of Tukaram that they may have started with.

It may be worthwhile to ask what I myself have been doing with Tukaram all these years and try to give a candid answer.

In retrospect, I have just gone through the vast body of Tukaram's work again and again, marked its leitmotifs, followed its major thematic strands and the often invisible but always palpable autobiographical thread. Each time, I have discovered something new. Some *abhang* or another that I had not noticed earlier has regularly exploded in my face. Tukaram's exquisite mastery of his medium has stunned me again and again.

This is the way I view my source-text—with absolute and unashamed reverence. These are the bases of my present selection and presentation of translations. No reference to the source-text or to any other works is necessary for the reader of this book. Quite simply, these are poems in English worked out by a twentieth century poet who is no relation of Tukaram. Tukaram himself did not write any of these poems in English, a language he did not know of in all probability. Translations of poetry are speculations about missing poets and lost poetry. They are done with dowsing-rods and non-scientific instruments. But their existence as entities in their own right cannot be disputed or denied.

A large number of friends and well-wishers have supported my Tukaram "project" since 1956. I would recall them in a chronological order, as far as possible, and also name the places where I worked then. The "support" came in various forms : discussion, advice, suggestions, references, books, information, criticism, encouragement, and even financial help whenever I had no income but was working full time on my translations.

In the first phase between 1956 and 1960 in Bombay, Bandu Vaze and Arun Kolatkar.

In the second phase between 1960 and 1963, Graham Tayar, Tom Bloor, and George Smythe in Addis Ababa, Ethiopia.

In the third phase between 1963 and 1970, Damodar Prabhu, Arvind Krishna Mehrotra, Sadanand Rege, K. Shri Kumar, A.B. Shah, and G.V. Karandikar, in Bombay.

In the fourth phase between 1970 and 1975 in Bombay, Adil Jussawala, who continued to back me all the way, all the time, ever since.

Between 1975 and the end of 1977 in Iowa City and other parts of the U.S.A., Daniel Weissbort, Burt Blume, Skip and Bonny O'Connell, William Brown, Angela Elston, A.K Ramanujan, Eleanor Zelliott, Margaret Case, Jayanta Mahapatra.

Between 1978 and 1983 in Bombay and parts of Europe, Gunther D. Sontheimer, Lothar Lutze, Orban Otto, Guy Deleruy.

Between 1983 and 1985, Ashok Vajpeyi, Shrikant Varma in Bhopal and New Delhi.

Between 1985 and 1990, mostly in Pune except for two visits to Europe, I brought this book into its present shape with significant and sustained help from Adil Jussawala, Anne Feldhaus, Gunther D. Sontheimer, Lothar Lutze, G.M. Pawar, A.V. Datar, Prakash Deshpande, Chandrashekhar Jahagirdar, Rajan Padval, Namdeo Dhasal, Anil and Meena Kinikar, Philip Engblom, Shridharbuva Moré, and Sadanand Moré in different ways.

I would like to recall here that it was my maternal grandfather, Kashinath Martand Gupte, who impressed upon my mind the greatness of Tukaram when I was only a child. My paternal grandmother, Sitabai Atmaram Chitre, gave me my first insight into *Bhakti*. My parents —my father in particular—regularly gave me books that were relevant to my work on Tukaram.

My greatest gratitude is towards my wife Viju, the first critical listener of my ideas as they evolve and of my poetry or translations. She is also the keeper of all that I possess or produce. Considering that the smallest scraps of paper with scribbled notes, scrawled messages, or intriguing squiggles have all been miraculously preserved by her in a nomadic life spent in three different continents during the last three decades, she deserves the world's greatest honour that I can personally bestow upon anyone.

This book is the product of the collective goodwill of all these people. All I own is the errors of omission and commission.

Pune
July 1991   *Dilip Chitre*

1. BEING A POET

I. BEING A POET

I was only dreaming
Namdeo and Vitthal
Stepped into my dream

"Your job is to make poems,"
said Namdeo,
"Stop fooling around."

Vitthal gave me the measure
And slapped me gently
To arouse me
From my dream
Within a dream

"The grand total
Of the poems Namdeo vowed to write
Was one billion,"
He said,
"All the unwritten ones, Tuka,
Are your dues."

If only you would
Give me refuge O Lord
To stay at your feet
In a line of saints.

I've already left behind
The world I loved.
Don't stand still:
It's your move now.

My caste is low;
My origins humble.
A little help from you
Will go a long way.

Thanks to Namdeo
You visited me
In a dream that left me
Poetry.

This is really extraordinary, O Hari.
You are supposed to relieve misery;
And here I am, your own devotee,
Whose house is haunted by poetry.

The more I excel in poems praising you,
The more my work seems flawed:
This is yet another amazing paradox.
Watchfulness is rewarded with anxiety.

Says Tuka, My Lord, it's just dawned on me:
To serve you is the ultimate difficulty.

Have I utterly lost my hold on reality
To imagine myself writing poetry?
I am sure your illustrious devotees,
All famous poets, will laugh at me.

Today, I face the toughest test of life:
Whereof I have no experience,
Thereof I have been asked to sing.

I am the innocent one asked to sin,
Without any foretaste of what I must commit
I am just a beginner, untutored in the art,
My Master Himself is unrevealed to me.

Illuminate, and inspire me, O Lord.
Says Tuka, my time is running out.

I scribble and cancel it again,
O heavenly critic, to pass your test.

I choose a word, only to change it,
Hoping to find one you'd like the best.

I beg your pardon again; and again;
Lord, let not my words go waste.

Says Tuka, please, talk back at least
So that this poem will have something to say.

Where does one begin with you?
O Lord, you have no opening line.
It's so hard to get you started.

Everything I tried went wrong.
You've used up all my faculties.

What I just said vanished in the sky
And I've fallen to the ground again.

Says Tuka my mind is stunned:
I can't find a word to say.

6

All I feel
Is God.
God is all
I believe.

Who brought
The world
Into being,
Makes me
Speak.

It wasn't I, who
Ordered
These words:
The idea is
His.

I wasn't trying
To become
A celebrity.
You'd be lucky
If you knew
What I mean.

Says Tuka, what I say
Must be true,
Because it starts
From Him.

I speak
And they think
It is poetry.
But I know
That He
Doesn't yet
Love me.

He doesn't
Respond to my poetry.
Narayana
Doesn't like it
At all.

Shame on my tongue
For speaking at all.

I know I was never good
At contemplation.
I just babble.

Says Tuka,
What an enormous
Waste!
O Lord of Pandhari,
What do you think
Of all these poems?

He who speaks
These poems through me
Is the only one who knows
How they were made.

Don't ask me.
I only carry them
Like His own load
And beg for bread
When I'm hungry.

He gave me the measure.
I just dole out His stuff
When He asks me.
I'm only the helper;
He's the Boss.
I'm His empty measure—
Filled with His grain;
Emptied by His order.

Pandurang is
My Maker;
And He is
The Giver.

The real world belongs
To the Parents.
A child only plays
The game
Mimicking the Parents' life.
His cows and buffaloes are real:
Mine are toys of clay.

Says Tuka,
Vitthal is the one
Who takes the
Words out of my mouth.

Some of you may say
I am the author
Of these poems.
But
Believe me
This voice
Is not my own.

I have no
Personal skill.
It is
The Cosmic One
Making me speak.

What does a poor fellow like me
Know of the subtleties of meaning?
I speak what Govind
Makes me say.

He has appointed me
To measure it out.
The authority rests
With the Master;
Not me.

Says Tuka, I'm only the servant.
See?
All this bears
The seal of His Name.

If, O Murari, You find it so hard
To give as abundantly as Your name promises,
I might as well somehow bide my time
Through thick and thin with a muzzled hymn.

Remember, it is the father who loses face
If the son is forced to bite the dust.

Without the salt of Your flavour, Says Tuka,
I cannot savour, even my own speech.

Whenever I address You,
I find Your back turned to me.
That is how I have learned
To understand Your feeling for me.

I do not get what I want from You,
Because I do not interest You.
Nor do You admire what I try to say,
Because I haven't got Your style.

You pretend to lend an ear
To what I am saying here and now.
But that's only a ploy to placate me;
For Your mind always seems to be elsewhere.

Says Tuka, I am watching Your every move:
I know all about Your restlessly wandering mind.

You do not even hear me out—
Then why should I look into empty shells?

Come, convince me where I am now;
And, O Lord, I'll do my best.

I have tried and tried all I could do.
How much longer must I wait for You?

Says Tuka, I've come to the end of my tether;
And, at Your feet
I totter.

You give away a little
To deny the lot:
My efforts seem to lack
The vigour to bear fruit.
My songs grind an empty hand-mill;
For you deny me the very grist.
Says Tuka, I rule my world, indeed.
My kingdom is an empty plate.

Don't think
It is self-pity.

I only feel
A great regret, because
I cannot save
Your reputation.

O Govinda
I do not want
To hear
Your Name
Defamed.

Says Tuka
I only wish
That the Lord's cause
Does not become
An embarrassment.

Why should I set up this shop
And mind its business?
Why should I advertise it
Making such a high pitch?

What's one small soul to you
That you would run to my rescue?
Isn't it futile to hope
That mouthing mere words would reveal you?

A king may not grant land to the landless:
But wouldn't he at least ensure
That his subjects get a meal?
After all a king must protect
The myth of his benevolence.

Don't you see the point, O Lord?
If you refuse me, says Tuka,
I'd be forced to close down your shop.

Well, then, God. Do you now
Expect me to feed myself only
And amuse the world
In the shape of your devotee?
Then say so for once
Unequivocally,
Because I cannot bear
This agony.

Or do you want me to write poems,
Compulsively
Turning out and fixing phrases?

Speak up, Narayana, says Tuka—
Am I to mind only my business
Even after having been
Ruined?

Mother
Look at me
With
Loving eyes
How dejected I am

Suckle
My soul
And
That's
No metaphor

I pine
For the truth
It's therefore I worry
About words

Pity me
Says Tuka, I am wrung
For my suffering
Is real

My task
Makes me
Gasp

My knowledge of you
Is reproduced
From
Learnt words:
It's like
A treasure
Extracted
From a mirror.

When will you become
Real for me
O Lord?
There's the pinch.

I sing;
I dance;
I eat, shit, breathe.
Like a flower
I contain
Your seed.
I'm losing time
God.
I cannot bear to wait.
I am eager
To receive
Your very
Being:
Says Tuka.

It was the right thing
That
Narayana did.
He made my jewels
Part of me.

Words came out
Like flashing gems:
Deep within me
He was the mine.

Words
Experience
The meaning
Of being
Unended.

Says Tuka—
Ananta is
The Infinite One.
My gift
Has no limit.

I don't know
The meaning
Of what I say.
It's not me
Speaking.
Try to understand me
O saints.
Don't lose your temper
So quick.
It is not me speaking.
It is Pandurang.
He has possessed me.
He has taken over this body.

What power to speak
Do I
An idiot
Have?
How can I speak
From beyond
The scriptures?
"Rama Krishna Hari
Mukunda Murari"
Is all I can manage
To mumble.

Says Tuka,
By the blessing
Of my Guru,
I am
On my feet.
All my burden
Is borne
By Pandurang.

Numismatic marvels
Fresh from the mint
Are here:
The secret vault
Of the Lord
Is laid open.

How can a slave explain
His Master's measure?
I am nobody.
He is the sovereign.

The master potter
Shapes them:
The pots he selects
Reach kitchens.

Says Tuka
Narayana is
The source of life:
He is the very
Being of light
Contained
In every ray.

I play this game
At His Blessed Feet:
This prosody
Has no dead end.

My Parent stands still
On the Brick
Watching me
Indulgently.

The words I speak
Are sacramental.
I speak
No heresy.

Says Tuka
I am the pool
Of growing feeling
Pandurang above
Is reflected in me.

21

I speak
As I have been taught
To speak.
I do not feel
As I speak.

There is no doubt now
O Lord.
I am good for nothing.

I have not become
A recluse.
I have not acted
As I resolved.

Says Tuka—
Neither is
My mind steady,
Nor are
My words
Controlled.

Insects in a fig
Cannot imagine
Worlds other than the fig.

There are so many fig-trees
In these woods:
And so many more
Vast clusters of stars.

To each his own is
Brahman
—Absolute Being.

How many such astral eggs
Will there be?

The Vast One bristles
With hairs
Of infinity.

Then there's the One who contains
Trillions of vast ones.

That same One is
Nanda's loved little son—
Krishna
—The Infant Bliss Infinite.

When Tuka experiences
That bliss,
God's poetry enters
His small head.

My first verse will thread the Three Worlds
I shall sing of my sacred Pandurang

My second verse will find otherness nowhere
In crowds and forests I find Pandurang

My third verse is fathomless space
The whole of God is forests and crowds

My fourth verse is a mill and everything's grist
I grind all into one being, Pandurang

My fifth verse is my home where I was born
I shall sing of Pandurang on and on

My sixth verse begins where the six scriptures end
And there is my Guru, Pandurang

My seventh verse is constant remembering
Pandurang in my eyes absolutely still

My eighth verse spans the twenty-eight Ages
Pandurang has stood still by the Chandrabhaga

My ninth verse spells the end of the grind
The whole world is freed from the wheel of death

My tenth verse is addressed to the Ten Avataras:
Says Tuka, I shall not return to any world again

My tongue being swift as lightning,
I vacillate without reaching the origin of being:
O Lord of Pandhari, that's where it hurts.
Who will understand the root of my suffering?

To them I have become worthy of worship.
I have become so vain, I cannot become free.
I cannot find the surest sign of you;
Says Tuka, my ego strangles me.

It was no use.
I spread
The word of God
In the world.
But my dialogue
With Him
Proved nothing.

In my eyes
He is empty.
He does not care
If one starves
To death.

I command
A literary style.
But
It leaves me cold.

I am an exile
In both my worlds.
I can neither lead
An average life
Nor be
With You.

Says Tuka, I wish
I knew it earlier,
Before this obsession
Destroyed me.

I am no Guru.
I rain like a cloud.
Listen.
O Saints
The sound you hear
Is the falling
Of rain.

It is baby-talk.
It comes from
God,
The beginning
Of speech.

Once
I got smelted
In His
Primordial mint.
Now I tumble out
As His coins.

Take a sip:
Says Tuka—
Drink your fill.
I have found
The spring.

My senses are at war
Among themselves.

Ears demand
What satisfies the tongue.

My hands,
My feet,
My forehead
All join the battle.

It's not a case
Where the ears listen quietly
To the mouth
That sings
Of Your properties.

Every sense demands
The Whole of You
To choose from.

Says Tuka,
O Narayana,
Yield.
For such
Is my frenzy.

To arrange words
In some order
Is not the same thing
As the inner poise
That's poetry.

The truth of poetry
Is the truth
Of being.
It's an experience
Of truth.

No ornaments
Survive
A crucible.
Fire reveals
Only molten
Gold.

Says Tuka
We are here
To reveal.
We do not waste
Words.

I pretend to laugh;
I pretend to weep;
I pretend to leap
At the Pretender.

Mine is a pretence;
Yours is a pretence;
Pretence bears the burden
Of pretending.

I pretend to sing;
I pretend to worship;
All pretence goes
Towards pretending.

The pretender savours;
The pretender renounces;
The ascetic pretends
The world is unreal.

Tuka, the pretender,
With pretended devotion,
Pretends his dialogue
With the Pretender.

2. BEING HUMAN

2. BEING HUMAN

I'm telling you
The truth
O saints.
I've sinned more
Than most.
I can't understand
Why
You find me
Worthy of love.

I am my own
Witness.
So trust
What my conscience
Tells me.
I have overcome
Nothing.
My fame is based
On mere hearsay.

Much harrowed by
A life full of hardships,
I stalled
Like a stubborn
Bullock,
That's had enough
Of whipping
And twisting of the tail,
While pulling
A hard plough.
I just dropped out.
And stayed still.

Soon what savings
I had
Vanished.
No.
I didn't
Make any sacrifice.
I didn't
Give it away in
Charity.

I cut myself
Off from my beloved wife;
My children,
My brother
Found me become
A sudden
Stranger.
I became
A wretched
Moron.

Ashamed to show
My face
To anyone,
I hid myself
In desolate corners;
Stayed alone
In unvisited places.
That's what they call
My reclusiveness now.

As for my sharing
Food with anyone,
The truth is:
I was always starving
And unable to bear
The pangs of hunger.
So, mercilessly,
I accepted
Any invitation
To a meal;
Chewing up
More than my share.

Finally,
My devotion
To this God:
The fact is
It's a habit
I inherited
From my father.
You see,
This deity's worship
Runs in the family.
It's no big deal.
Says Tuka,
Don't mistake it
For extraordinary
Bhakti.

It's all gone
To wrack and ruin.
We're all
Down and out.

Nobody
Claims us.
Lord
You are
In full spate.

My home
Lies shattered.
My very seat
Is destroyed.

Says Tuka
O God
Come closer
To me.

Where did it
Go wrong?
I was
Doing well.
What made me grab
This noose
That's around
My neck?

Now I'm tied
In too many
Knots.
I cannot
Move
Back
Or forth.

I have nothing
Left.
I am too deep
In debt.

My harvest
Has been
Looted.
My wife
And my children
Have to beg.

I borrow
Left and right.
Nothing
Seems enough.

Says Tuka,
It's best
I give up
All hope
And leave
All this
Where is
As is.

Where shall I go now?
What shall I eat?
With whose backing
Shall I live in this village?

The village chief
Is furious with me.
All the public
Hates my sight.

I plead with them.
But they won't listen.
I've lost all decency
They say.
Their council has
Convicted me.

It's no go.
According to
The powers that be
I'm burnt out.

Says Tuka,
It's no good
To remain
In such company.
I had better
Pack up
And go
In search
Of Vitthal.

Good for me God I am broke;
Good that this famine made it worse.
Suffering made me think of You
And I vomited this world.

Good for me Lord my wife's a shrew;
Good that I'm stripped in public view.
I am blessed that the whole world insults me;
Thank You, I've lost all property.

How nice it feels to be without any shame!
What a relief! Now I'm all Yours.
Good that I rebuilt Your ruined shrine
Instead of salvaging my shattered home.

Says Tuka, I'm glad I fasted on Your day
Starving has kept me stark awake.

Merciful Lord
What am I to do?

I cannot make
The ends meet.

Like a monkey
In a tree
I climb up
And down.

I thrust my hand
Where it shouldn't be
Only to get cursed
And kicked out.

Says Tuka—
From the beginning
To the end,
It's all gone wrong.

Advice to an Angry Wife : I

"Why me? This man renounces everything
About me. Has he lost
All sense of pleasure, then?

"He seems to be visited by all the thrills of life
And I'm left cheated of all I had.

"Whose wife am I supposed to be?
I work my arse off for *his* family.

"What can I feed these starving children?
They are so hungry, they could eat *me*.

"Why don't they die? That would take care of them.

"He wouldn't let a thing remain in this house.
He hasn't left me even a lump of cowshit
I can plaster my mud floor with.'

Says Tuka, the stupid bitch works too hard
And goes on groaning without pausing to think.

Advice to an Angry Wife : II

"A sackful of grain is delivered at our door.
But this bastard won't let his own children eat.

"He distributes it to the whole town.
I suspect he himself eats it too."

Says Tuka, you stupid bitch!
Don't you understand that the deeds of the past
Can never be stored?

Advice to an Angry Wife : III

"Now there's nothing left for you to eat.
Will you eat your own children?
My husband is God-crazy!

"See how he beats his own head?
See how he wears garlands!
He has stopped minding his shop.

"His own belly is full
While the rest of us must starve

"Look at him, striking cymbals
And opening his grotesque mouth
To sing to his God in his shrine!'

Says Tuka, be patient, my woman!
This is only the beginning!

Advice to an Angry Wife : IV

"Good that he's gone away today!
I've got all I want.

"Now I can eat
All the bread in peace
With or without gravy!

"I am tired of shooting off my mouth
At this stone-deaf man!"

Says Tuka, my wife
Just loves to curse me.

Advice to an Angry Wife : V

"He can't stand the idea of work;
He is used to getting free meals.

"As soon as he wakes, he starts to sing.
All hell breaks loose after that.

"These fellows are the living dead.
They have no conscience to prick.

"They've turned a blind eye to their families.
They have deserted their homes.

"Their wives twist and turn for them
While they crush their lives with a stone."

Says Tuka, that's a good one, my wife!
Here! I've written it down!

Advice to an Angry Wife : VI

Pandurang, the noble collector of revenue,
Gives us our share of what we reap.

He asks us to repay seventy per cent
Of what we've owed in the past;
And we've so far cleared only ten per cent.

Sitting on a cot in our living-room,
He points to all our possessions:
The storage bin, the pots and pans, the cattle we own.

If I bargain and argue with Him, he keeps His cool.
He says, "Just pay up all your dues and what you reap
Will be all yours."

Says Tuka, my dear wife, what shall I do?
I don't know where to hide without paying my due.

Advice to an Angry Wife : VII

I think about it and realize that
After all, this is His own kingdom.
Who would protect me from Him?
Where else can we go to escape Him?

The front yard is wide open and the backyard, too.
In what stables or cow-sheds can we hide?
His henchmen will chase us wherever we go.

I kick myself for becoming one of His share-croppers.
Now I can never get out of His clutches.

Says Tuka, it cannot be helped.
One has to remain here and live
On His terms—not our own.

Advice to an Angry Wife : VIII

What can I do? It's my destiny catching up with me.
He gave me life Who gave me a conscience.
Nobody can say that this is my own doing.
It was God's order.

He freed me from bondage and set me abroad
As a beggar. And yet He continues to stalk me.

This God made me drink water from the dried shell of a gourd,
And forced me to live on the leaves of plants growing wild.

Says Tuka, I am perfectly aware
That He has no trace of kindness in Him;
He is going to lick me clean.

Advice to an Angry Wife : IX

Good people will have a great regard for you;
And the world will view you with growing respect.

Think of your cattle as dead
And of your pots and pans as stolen by a thief.
Think of your children as though they were never born.
Give up all desires and make your mind
Hard as Indra's warhead.
Spit out all mean pleasures
And receive pure bliss.

Says Tuka, you will be rid of great turmoil
Once you break free from the bonds of this world.

Advice to an Angry Wife : X

What gives me the strength to spurn all bodily pleasure?
Woman, you have become blind to the great fact.

Look at me! My hunger and my thirst have been stilled.
My disquietude has been calmed at its origin.

The wealth that people prize more than their life
Makes less sense to me now than a piece of gravel.

All good people are my kin;
And my love of companionship
Equals my love of solitude.
Being one with all is being beyond all bonds.

Says Tuka, Pandurang is with us
To enjoy and to suffer.

When my father died
I was too young to understand;
I had not to worry
About the family then.

Vithu, this kingdom is Yours and mine.
It's not the business of anyone else.

My wife died:
May she rest in peace.
The Lord has removed
My attachment.

My children died:
So much the better.
The Lord has removed
The last illusion.

My mother died
In front of my eyes.
My worries are all over
Says Tuka.

Alone I am

Nobody's darling

Nothingness
Strikes me
With terror

I dread
These hordes
Of beasts

Pandurang!

I panic

Darkness
Blocks me

I'm paralysed

I'll stumble
Into thickets

I'll be pierced
By thorns

Desolate

At the forking
Of a million
Paths

I've lost my way

I shudder

Says Tuka

The road
You showed me
Is my Guru

But
Pandurang!

You are so
Far.

I am bankrupt
And God
Is ruined.

This is no time
For eloquence.

One has to probe
One's mind.

I've wound up
My business.

Says Tuka—
God!
Just let me sit
Where I am.

This experience
Never leaves me:

Those behind me
Those ahead of me
None of them have peace.

Says Tuka
Life is the root
Of all anguish.

I cannot
Give up food.
I cannot
Withdraw to the woods.

Therefore,
O Narayana
I seek
Solace in You.

I have no right
To read or write
Says Tuka
I have only lived a little
And it's all still
A puzzle.

53

The Cripple : I

I am crippled
O my Lord
I have neither hands nor legs
What I am sitting on is
Sliding at a crazy speed
It heads straight
Into fences, thickets, stumps of trees
I am an orphan
And nobody cares for me

Sliding in and out of all these
Doors of birth, doors of death
I am tired and sunk, tired and sunk
I cannot yet find one compassionate soul
To free me from this painful ride

O reveal to me the Ruler of Pandhari
The same Hari that all the saints sing of
The one who restores the limbs of the maimed

"O my fathers, my mothers,
O parents of all orphans!
Give me some food," I constantly beg,
As each one turns me away.

Helpless but hounded by hope
I continue to slide all the way

I cannot tell what's wrong, what's right
I do not know what my crimes were
I hover about life with a lost memory
As a moth unable to reach the flame

O saints, O great ones!
Give me your gift of life.
I have come very far, yearning for a cure,
Says Tuka, I have come to your feet
By a rare stroke of fortune; and I beg,
"Give me relief."

The Cripple : II

I have just stumbled into this territory.
I am dressed like a stranger.
This is not my country.
I could not settle down in any one place.

So what do I own?
What can I possess?
I am in an alien land.
I have lost my legs
And I am blind.

Now O Lord I have none:
No ancestors, no descendants.
I surrender myself into your care.
Let these saints look after me.

I am afraid of taking this path;
For many have taken it and never come back.
I haven't seen them or heard of them since.
I am sitting at the very brink
Thinking only of You.

Pity me O Lord!
I have been hungry
Ever since I lost my home.
I have wandered without stopping anywhere.
I have visited all the 840,000 villages
That *karma* compels a man to go through.

I am tired.
You are my last stop,
My final place of rest.

I doubt now if anyone would
Grant me salvation anymore.
I have become a most notorious beggar.

Therefore, O Generous One, I appeal to You alone.
Only You can satisfy my monstrous hunger,
With a morsel of Your mercy.

I have no past merit to bank on.
I've lost my wife, children, my every belonging.
I have cut off every bond of life.

O Lord!
This was indeed my destiny.
Says Tuka,
Decide my fate.
I am entirely in Your hands

57

I was held captive
In a nightmare.
It was over
And I woke up.
It became unreal.

Why was I
Begging You
To reveal to me
My identity?
What's a king,
A nobleman,
Or a pauper
In a dream?

But the pain
Of the dream
Still lived
In me.
As I woke up,
I opened
My eyes
In pain.

I was awake
But stunned
By the pain
I dreamt.
It was so real
That I remained
Speechless.
Says Tuka,
Thank God,
The saints
Broke the spell.

3. BEING A DEVOTEE

The Image of Vithoba : I

In an exquisite trance
He stands on the Brick
Arms akimbo
Hands on hips

Sweet basil beads
Garland His neck
A yellow silk garment
Girdled around His loins
I love His trance
His forever stance

Crocodile-shaped rings
Gleam at His ears
The *Kaustubha* stone
Glows at His throat

Says Tuka, for me
This is absolute bliss
The loving eyes are mine
The loved face His

The Image of Vithoba : II

From now on
Let me remain in this trance
My sight, my mind
Tempted beyond time

I shall shut my life
To enclose His form
I shall feel Him in my body
To worship Him

He will enter my soul
And make it still
Peaking
Into an absolute spire

Says Tuka,
O my bonny Vithoba
Let me lie prostrate
At Your feet.

The Image of Vithoba : III

O what kind of Lord are You
Who remains beyond my sight:
Beautiful, lavish, blue?

Four-armed; graced
By a single garland;
A streak of musk
On the forehead;
Holding a conch-shell, a discus, a mace;
Wearing the *Vaijayanti* necklace;
Rings gleaming
In both the ears.

Says Tuka:
O Merciful Maya,
Mother of all appearance!
Pandurang!
Show me
Your feet.

The Image of Vithoba : V

O Hari—
Level-eyed,
Even-footed,
Symmetrically stanced
On the Brick—
Be the sole object
Of my attention forever.

I need not chase
Any other
Phenomenon that tricks
And breaks the heart.

The status of Brahma,
Or any other god,
That you dangle in front
Of the eyes of seekers
Is not for me.

Says Tuka, I know,
There's the rub:
Karma perishes
Along with life.

Lord, my heart is
Full of Your footprints.
You are my path.

We are blind.
You are our legs.
You are our thought.
You are our walk.

My senses have been blanked.
My mind stays still
Not by my own
Will.

You have made me see
Beyond good and evil.
You have made me transcend
Matter, life, and mind.

Says Tuka:
I have surrendered myself;
And, O Kind One,
The glory is Yours alone.

"Stupid ones, smart ones, learned ones
—All are crazy for You.

"But none of them grasp You.
They'd stew in hell.

"Meanwhile, the lame one crosses the mountain.
The deaf-mute echoes You.

"The sinner attains grace.
The wicked one ceases to harm."

Says Tuka,
He is everywhere.
He plays the game
He watches from a distance.

Horizontal He is:
He is vertical.
Down and across,
One intense light.

God is not uniform:
What makes Him
Homogeneous
Is purity of the heart.

Arguments about
His unity or duality
Are condemned
To continue.

Says Tuka,
You must come
Out of your involvements
And vested interests
To grasp Him
Whole.

Wherever I look
I find erect
The very pith and core
Of the sky:

His image is pressed
To the depth of my eye:
The more I absorb Him,
The more He is compressed.

My mind is alert:
Ready to receive Him,
My vision is emptied
Of all else.

Says Tuka,
And now I have
God
For company.

Who is the one
That conceives?
Who is the one
That is born?
O Benevolent One
I cannot fathom
Your love of form.

Who is the one
That asks?
Who is the one
That gives?
O Benevolent One
I cannot fathom
Your form of love.

Who is the one
That experiences?
Who creates
That experience?
O Benevolent One
I cannot fathom
Your form of love.

Who is the one
That manifests?
Who is the unmanifested
One?
O Benevolent One
I cannot fathom
Your love of form.

Says Tuka, it is
You everywhere
And You are everything
Other than You.

Let this lump in my throat
Smother me.
Let it explode my heart.
O Vitthal
Let me take You
By storm.

Let me cry.
Do not let this flow stop.
Let me bristle
With bliss.

Says Tuka,
I want no less
Than a complete
Embrace.

I look for You
O Keshava
With the wistful eyes
Of a married daughter
Leaving her parental home:

I search
You
With the eyes
Of a baby missing
Its mother:

Parted from water,
A fish twists
Like a tortured
Tuka.

Because Your form is beyond the reach
Of speech and mind, I have to measure You
With my own devotion.
Since You are immeasurable by definition, O Anant,
I map You with my endless passion.

Yoga cannot grasp You, sacrificial rites cannot get You,
You do not yield to penance, the senses cannot touch You,
Knowledge cannot discover You; and so,

Says Tuka, O Keshav,
You must take what I give
With innocent feeling.

Wind up what you know.
Only your feeling counts there.

Follow just one thing.
Pandurang knows everything.

Do not argue the pros and the cons.
It's a sheer waste of time.

Says Tuka, they wear themselves out
Who speak without any feeling.

Know nothing without Pandurang;
Doubt will only exhaust you.

Even if you remember Him by any other name,
Your Father understands why you pine.

Praise Him and you are no more vain;
Listen to His story and wishes come true.

Says Tuka, you will spontaneously overflow
With the feeling of love without end.

Life in this world is unreal
Only Hari's name is real
Without Hari
It's all a mere function of the senses

A vow of silence is unreal
As unreal as a dream of hallucinating
Meditation without Hari
Is bound to perish

Deductions made without Hari
Are unreal theses
He is a dead person
Whose mind has no place for Hari

Says Tuka
Will one thing: Hari
And you'll instantly be
In Vaikunth

You are my mother
I rest in Your shade
For You I wait
Pandurang

You are my only one
My big one, my small one
You are the only kin
I have

Says Tuka, my soul
Rests in You
All else
Is emptiness

To hell with knowledge
To hell with wisdom
Let my feeling settle
On the feet of Vitthal

To hell with decorum
To hell with discretion
Let my mind stand still
At the feet of Vitthal

To hell with repute
To hell with fame
Let my mind be absorbed
In Vitthal

To hell with the body
To hell with its bonds
Let the supreme bliss be
Always at my throat

Says Tuka,
This is all
You will distill
O my mind
Avail
Of Vitthal

How many layers of pleasure are to be peeled
To reveal the innermost pith of pleasure?
The Vaishnavas' pleasure is the image of pure bliss:
It waits in the courtyard of their own houses.

There, the holy basil plant flourishes in its little tower of clay
The earth is freshly sprayed with water;
Squares are drawn on the ground with coloured dust; garla
hung;
Such a festive setting makes Him break into dance.

Spangled, bejewelled, wearing a garland of holy basil beads,
He is forever present there in His sacred insignia.
His immortal name flows ceaselessly from their lips.
The dust in their dishevelled hair is touched by God.

Says Tuka, the devotees' passion for God reaches
A pitch beyond any craving for transcendence.

From Tukaram's Letter to Vitthal

With the saints who are going on a pilgrimage to Pandharpur
I send Him this message:

"Your servant
Tuka
Beseeches You :
Do not forget me.

"At Your great gate
I remain
Your everlasting
Broom.

"My mind
And my body
Fit Your feet
As shoes.

"My mouth is open
Like a spittoon
For You
To spit in
Betel-leaf juice.

"I offer
My body
As a pot
To receive
O Lord
Your shit.

"I am
The soil
Touched by
Your feet.

"Says Tuka—
O Lord of Pandharpur
Do not ever
Treat me
As anything
Else"

Pandharpur : I

Happiness fell into Pandhari.
Pundalik kept it in place.

O my elders, run for it now.
Taste it with your own tongue.

Make just one trip there.
You won't have to wander ever after.

Pack up your attachments bag and baggage.
Make a scramble for Pandharpur.

It's not a bad idea to reach there in time
—While you are still alive!

Says Tuka, listen to this peasant's plea:
Reach there and reap it, don't dilly-dally.

Pandharpur : II

This mine was opened in ancient times.
People have been digging it long since.
But its treasure hasn't depleted.

Grand masters, great sages, able initiates—all
Have cared to preserve its inner resources.

The One who landed on His feet into this world
Is its landmark. Pundalik revealed Him to all.

Says Tuka, I went there as a helpless soul.
Now I've made myself a small fortune.

Pandharpur : III

The Great Ghost of Pandhari
Pounces upon every one who passes by.

That forest is haunted by many spirits.
Whoever enters it finds it maddening.

O do not ever go there—you!
Nobody who goes in ever comes back.

Only once did Tuka go to Pandhari:
He hasn't been born ever since.

Pandharpur : IV

The Thug has arrived in Pandhari.
He will garrotte His victim with the cord of love.

He's robbed the whole world before.
He takes His victims no one knows where.

He's raised His arms
To grab your attention.

He's decamped from Vaikunth
To hunt in Pandhari.

It was Pundalik who gave this Robber
A foothold in Pandhari.

Says Tuka, let's all go there
And put Him under arrest.

Pandharpur : V

The ship docks
On the bank of the Chandrabhaga.

It is laden with vast treasure.
O Saints! Help yourselves.

The tide of Hari's name is receding.
The mast is being furled.

Tuka is Vitthal's favourite porter.
God helps him with his burden.

Pandharpur : VI

Now to Pandhari we go
To lie prostrate at Vithoba's feet

There on the bank of Chandrabhaga
At Pandharpur we shall dance

Where all the saints crowd
There we shall go and touch their feet

Says Tuka, we are the sacrificial beast
To be happily trampled under all those feet

Pandharpur : VII

You have evolved so long
To be finally born as man,
Now you must get
Related to God.

You must act
In your own interest now:
Stop chasing
Meaningless meanings.

Give up your bodily concerns
And those fantasies of a good time.
The road to Pandhari
Lies straight ahead.

Go to Pandhari
And have a great time.
It's so good to see Him
Standing on the Brick.

On the base of that Brick
Bliss Itself stands tall.
Tuka dances to the beat of the chant
Singing His name.

Pandharpur : VIII

Those who keep time with Pandhari
Are pilgrims of eternity

Those who speak constantly of Vitthal
Cease to belong to the material world

Look! Here come the servants of Hari!
From guilts they'll make you instantly free.

The body is swept by the glad tide:
Blend into His colour, dance, go wild!

Their bodies smeared with *gopichandan* paste!
Tulsi-bead necklaces adorning them!

The weak, the poor, the helpless—all
Find Him: as much as they badly need;
Says Tuka, loosen the tight purse-strings of your hearts
To receive the Lord like mint-fresh cash.

Pandharpur: IX

Why make mountains of efforts in atonement?
Why bear the crushing burden of sorrow?

Why wander in distant countries, O seeker?
Why chase a reward in the remote future?

Why worship a multitude of diverse deities?
You have it right here if you seek no profit.

Why sweat so much for salvation?
In Pandhari it costs you nothing!

Says Tuka, sing His praise.
He delivers it at your door.

Pandharpur : X

Over there you will see
A crowd of endless pilgrims
And a sea of waving banners

The King of Pandharpur will arrive any moment
These are the sure signs He's getting closer

My heart leaps, my eyes cannot wait,
My arms are already open

A vast chorus is raising His slogan,
Vishnu's armies are greeting their Chief

Tuka empties his heart
To contain the whole scene

God's Own Dog : I

I've come to Your door
Like a dog looking for a home
O Kind One
Don't drive me away

I refuse to leave Your door
Don't force me out

I have no shame
I lick Your feet

Says Tuka,
O Narayana
You look
So promising!

God's Own Dog: II

Dogs are possessive
About their own place
They can't stand
Even a whiff of strangers
They'd tear them to pieces
Turning a home
Into a battlefield

Tuka won't let
Anyone near
Except
In the company
Of God

God's Own Dog : III

Once I chase someone
I chase him
Out of this world

Then I come back
To Your feet
And hide
Till You send me out
Again

The moment this dog
Smells a stranger
He scrambles
To attention

Says Tuka,
My Master's trained me hard
I am allowed to eat
Only out of his own
Hand

God's Own Dog : IV

Like a dog
Lying at Your door
"Hari! Hari!"
I bark Your name

I bark
I get up
I sit down again
But never
O Gopal
Would I leave
Your feet

Says Tuka,
"I know,
My master's weakness:
He just loves
To fondle
His pet!"

God's Own Dog : V

I am bound
By a chain of love
And I bark
Only when I must

O Keshav
My King
I am
Your watchdog
By appointment

I am aware
Of who comes
Who goes
And where
I know who's taking
A forbidden turn

Says Tuka, I watch out
For evil
And keep it
Off limits

God's Own Dog : VI

Pamper a dog
And it's spoilt for good
It'll loiter at your feet
And get in your way

That's how I've become
With You
Staying too damn close
All the time

I come wagging my tail
When You eat Your dinner

Says Tuka,
O Lord
I don't even notice
If You are annoyed!

God's Own Dog : VII

God just loves His dog.
I am no slave
I am His pet
He's taught me
To sit by His side
To be
Where He is

I'm allowed
Nothing more
Than to growl
Now and then

Says Tuka,
When He
Caresses me
I feel
Almost
Like a saint

God's Own Dog : VIII

Fed up of eating leftovers
The dog gets bold
And tries his master's toe

The master's quick to understand
He feeds him morsels of hot food

He feeds him lovingly
From His own plate
And that's how
He pampers His pet

Says Tuka,
I'm too old a dog now
I've no such appetites left.

4. BEING IN TURMOIL

When He comes
Out of the blue
A meteorite
Shattering your home
Be sure
God is visiting you

When a catastrophe
Wipes you out
And nothing remains
But God and you
God is visiting you

When your language
Is stripped naked
Never to be clothed
In falsehood again
Be sure
God is visiting you

When your humanness
Is rent and riven
Never to be pieced
Together again
Be sure
God is visiting you

When you are
Beyond all hope
When you call
Nothing your own
Be sure
God is visiting you

When you are robbed
Of the whole world
And your voice
Becomes eloquent
Be sure
God is visiting you.

See how God has
Grabbed the whole of him!
Tuka is raging
Like God Himself.

It's a scandal

Big people
And small
Slander me

I've lost
My community

All doors are
Slammed
In my face

This is my lot
I accept it

Says Tuka
God has done
What's best for me

Let us go to God's own town
God will give us relief

Let us tell God what we've gone through
He will set our craving at ease

Let us give ourselves into His charge
For God is the ocean of bliss

Let us remain close to God
Let us stay put at His feet

The beloved babies of God, Says Tuka, we are.

We fit You in a frame to worship You,
Though You contain the fourteen universes.
We display You to show our pleasure
Though You have no definition or form.
We sing songs addressed to You,
Though You are way beyond words.
We put garlands around your neck,
Though You are apart from all action.
Says Tuka, O God, become limited
To pay me a little attention.

You have no fixed address

You raise
All sorts of shacks
And shanty towns

You are found
In the strangest of places

And usually
You are sitting glum
In your corner

You are neither awake
Nor asleep

You seem to be starving
But you have
No appetite

Says Tuka
O Lord
I will not ask
How you are
I'll just
Describe you

I'll fight
You
And I'm sure
I'll hit you
In the tenderest spot.

Lord
You are a lizard
A toad
And a tiger
Too

And at times
You are
A coward
Frantically
Covering
Your own arse

When you face
A stronger-willed
Assault
You just
Turn tail
You attack
Only the weak
Who
Try to run away

Says Tuka
Get
Out of my way
You are
Neither man
Nor woman
You aren't even
A thing.

Who will help me to reason this out?
Who will raise my sagging morale?
I am no well-read philosopher or pundit,
I am just a casteless destitute.
In this anarchic Age of Kali
The sharp ones will pounce on me for singing Your praises.
I am in this tormenting double-bind:
To sing of You or not to sing.
Says Tuka, now that all people are distanced from me,
Should I continue to be or end my being?

When we go wrong, O Pandurang,
You are so quick to punish us:
Why don't you concede us our rights?

When other seekers sought you, you tricked them by giving
Gifts of magical powers as bribe:
Let us get the record straight,
I'm not that sort of beggar.

Why should I get increasingly entangled in this world?
Just to satisfy my own ego like them?
I have preserved the purity of my pledge
Not to be tempted by anything else.

Says Tuka, from the outset, I expected nothing from you
So that my desire should not become the last barrier between us.

O gracious one, don't bear me any grudge.
I'll tease you with praise and torture you with irony:

I do not dare to think of your limitations
And I do not know how to serve you best

You are not finite, you have no form,
You are not visible, you do not change,
You have no property, you are pure being and awareness,
O exquisite one!

How eagerly have you grabbed all the best epithets
For yourself! And how mean you are
When it comes to your wretched devotee?
Says Tuka, O Govinda, let my head
Rest forever at your feet!

Promise me O Lord that Your head
Will lie at my feet

Such a topsy-turvy sight
Will surely cause me great delight

What other gift of greater value
Can one receive from You?

Do not refuse O Vitthal, says Tuka,
Set an example.

Finally I have found out your true character, O Lord!
You trick me into serving you.

Mind you, though, my difficulties are only
A burden for you and all these saints:

For you made me eloquent only to praise yourself
Now come out with some real proof.

Look! I am a grocer by profession.
You can't cheat me at a bargain.

Says Tuka, how do you expect me to dance in ecstasy
Before experiencing you?

Unrestrained by reason or any sense of decency,
You love to fight in the open streets of the bazaar.

You deal with only those
Who become like you.

You rob everyone
Of his last strip of clothing.

Says Tuka, O hoodlum,
You are nobody's chum.

This whole transaction is a fraud.
I will have nothing more to do with you.

You do not operate under one name.
You have thousands of aliases.

When one tries to seek your true identity,
You begin to play hide and seek.

Says Tuka,
You are full of mischief.

I will not utter your name again.
I will not work as you ask any more.

The more words I use, the more absurd this becomes.
I speak of your attributes and find flaws of my own speech.

Who is going to make all those trips to your house and back
Any more? Certainly not me!

Says Tuka, haven't I got all that I want
Right here with me?

Aren't you supposed to be the indivisible One?
Why, then, should I regard you as Alone?

Small ants and big ants, indeed!
You play such melodramatic games with your audience!

You are the limit!
So: do I now begin to show my own annoyance?

Says Tuka, the truth about you is in my own heart.
How do you expect to get out of there?

Lord, if you wanted to be left alone,
Why did you make those false passes at me?

After giving me a fiery sermon and driving me out,
Now you have shut your door and locked it on me.

You have turned out all the lights and darkened your house;
And you have even posted a guard at your door.

Says Tuka, I hope that you understand well,
I would serve you only till you inspire some fear.

I cannot bear the day; I cannot bear the night.
I am so much ashamed that I cannot even admit it.

I waste my words like the wind; you do not even taste them.
Your indifference humiliates me; I seethe with rage.

My mind cries to itself;
It chokes; and then it is spent.

Says Tuka, after all, You are omniscient!
How can I argue my hopeless case?

Now I really feel that I am fallen
O Lord, I have gone through it all

The distance between us is closed now
Deal directly with me

Why do you need a third one as witness
When we stand face to face?

Says Tuka, I died even as I was speaking to you
And you have realized it only just now

Now I have understood well
That One must become like Him
Whom One seeks:

You are beyond desire, O Narayana!
And I am just like You.

It is like a thief
Against the Master Thief:
Who will rob whom?
We are testing our skills.

Says Tuka, I fight with myself:
I fear no loss of life.

I never knew what to ask of you
You never did me any good

Why do you close your eyes now?
Why do you seal your lips?

What sort of dumb God are you
Who needs to be told what ought to be done?

Says Tuka, I have already met my worst
You knew it was coming, yet what did you do?

I spoke to you with the intimacy of a child
Don't you speak back to me such harsh words

Forgive me my mischief, O excellent master,
Teach me what you consider right

When a child tries to grasp a flame in its hand,
It is innocent: it's the mother who pulls it back

Says Tuka, O lord, you are an expert at leaving
Each one to face the music on his own

I shouldn't speak, but the situation compells me
The whole world goes hoarse appealing to you

O conjuror who has spread out this vast show
I know you are really a beggar worth nothing

Having become your dependents, we have become shameless
And therefore we put up with you

We do not know how you will contrive
To end all this clamour created by us

Says Tuka, you are fair indeed! my Lord,
You accept my service without any response

You haven't yet paid me my price, my wages due,
Let us see who wins when it's time to settle our accounts

As for me, I am so desperate, I have staked my whole life,
I wonder if you have such guts

So far, O Hari, you have cheated millions at this game
But I am something else, I won't let you escape

I suffered a lot before I came across you
And learnt your name and identity

That was the mistake I made just once, says Tuka,
Now I am going to square with you

Lord, pay no heed to the words that I use;
Listen to my begging voice.

What force can one use at Your almighty feet?
We are slaves seeking Your mercy.

What do I care for this world?
It was good as long as it lasted for me.

I try to get closer with eager words:
I repeat Your name to reach You by rote.

I feel you will fulfil my hope in the end;
Therefore I am obsessed by You.

Says Tuka, all that I love is right here:
I want to behold Your resplendent face.

Lord, You could become sixteen thousand lovers
To the sixteen thousand wives you are reputed to have had.
I am just one and you are not even one for me!

Maybe such discriminatory behaviour befits you
Since, after all, you are Almighty.

Such is your wont! You would of course prefer
The possession of their maidenheads.

Says Tuka, O Pandurang, distinguish me
From the objects of your promiscuity.

A warrior on the warpath does not look back.
Give me that sort of courage.

Worldly life has alienated me from You.
Bless me, God!

I carry the weapon of Your Name
That's all I am armed with.

Says Tuka, were I to retreat from here
It will be a matter of shame, You know!

Lord, You could become sixteen thousand lovers
To the sixteen thousand wives you are reported to have had
I am just one, and you are not even one for me!

Maybe such discriminatory behaviour befits you
Since, after all, you are Almighty

Such is your wont! You would of course prefer
The possession of their maidenheads

Says Tuka, O Pandurang, distinguish me
From the objects of your promiscuity

A warrior on the warpath does not look back.
Give me that sort of courage.

Worldly life has alienated me from You.
Bless me, God!

I carry the weapon of Your Name
That's all I am armed with.

Says Tuka, were I to retreat from here
It will be a matter of shame. You know!

5. BEING IN TIME AND PLACE

n this Age of Evil poetry is an infidel's art:
The world teems with theatrical performers.

Their craving for money, lusting for women, and sheer reproduction
Define their values and priorities:
And what they mouth has no connection with their own being.

Hypocrites! They pretend such concern for where the world is going,
Talk of self-sacrifice, which is far from their minds.

They cite Vedic injunctions but can't do themselves any good.
They are unable to view their own bodies in perspective.

Says Tuka a torturesome death awaits
All those whose language is divorced from being.

The Brahmin

The *brahmin* who flies into a rage at the touch of a *mahar*
—That's no *brahmin*.
The only absolution for such a *brahmin*
Is to die for his own sin.

He who refuses to touch a *chandal*
Has a polluted mind.

Says Tuka, a man is only as chaste
As his own belief.

115

With a bizarrely painted face, glowering,
He flashes lights to dazzle their sight.

Tells his disciples, "This is beatitude!"
And indeed they are bamboozled.

He smothers the flame of the light itself!
His teaching begins when the sun goes down.

Drawing mystic squares on the ground, decorating them too,
He worships occult designs.

Placing lamps in all four corners and behind curtains
He assumes a posture and demonstrates *tantric* gestures.

As an oblation, he wants to be offered sweets—
Nothing short of a divine feast!

His preaching over, time to start the feast!
Forget about sipping water from the palm of the hand at the end c
the mea

Committing sacrilege is his means of livelihood:
He sends his followers into the bottomless pit.

He makes them break the vows of body, mind, and speech:
He teaches them to recite only the Guru's name.

He has corrupted the doctrine of the self-beyond-the self:
In the name of the Guru, he is only indulging himself!

Sacred precepts are wiped out; the Vedas are sunk;
The teachings of the scriptures are lost beyond a trace.

He has lost the control of his breath as taught in Yoga;
He cannot control his senses or follow observances.

116

Asceticism is destroyed; the worship of Hari is disturbed;
This maniac has spread only sin.

Says Tuka, may his Guruhood end up in a creek of shit!
He has condemned his ancestors to Hell!

The Great Mother of the Shakta
Is a Sow wallowing in shit by the roadside:
He is so habituated to it
He would chase his own mother for the sake of shit

The Great Mother of the Shakta is a she-donkey
Who goes braying all the way to the village-entrance
Says Tuka, to describe the slut
Would be to foul up one's own mouth

The Ascetic

Growing long shags of hair
He walks haughtily clasping a hooked iron rod.

He must not miss a single meal;
He must compulsively curse all people;
What wisdom can such an ascetic have?

He must consume a lot of *bhang*, and opium, and tobacco;
But his hallucinations are perpetual.

Says Tuka, such a man, who has forefeited everything,
Has lost Pandurang forever.

I know no trick
To lure the public.
I can only sin of You
And praise Your goodness.
I work no miracles,
I wake no dead.
I have no hordes of disciples
To advertise my selflessness.
I am not the lord of a monastery
Thriving on grants of land.
I run no God-shop
To worship personal profit.
I command no spirits,
Nor hold any seances.
I am no teller of tales from the Puranas
Split between profession and practice.
I am no wretched pundit
Splitting Vedantic hairs.
I burn no lamps to raise
The Mother Goddess with shrill praise.
I swing no rosary
To gather fools around me.
I am no warlock
To bewitch, to magnetize, to fix, to kill.
Tuka is not like any of these
Crazed citizens of hell.

People display their own daughters like goods for sale
And marry them off to the highest bidder

This is the done thing in this Age of the Infidel Kali
Virtue is the beggar, vice is the king

Drop-outs from decency
Brahmins lie and steal

They have wiped off the sacred mark on the forehead
And they now wear trousers and leather things

They occupy seats of power
And mete out injustice to the poor

They write inventories of the pantry
Thinking of ghee, oil, and soap

They become the hired servants of the corrupt
And take a beating whenever they err

The ruler exploits his own subjects
The warrior strikes at the suffering masses

The merchants and the labourers
Were born low to begin with

It is all a superficial show
Hiding the ugliness within

Says Tuka, have you dozed off, my Lord?
Run to their rescue, be quick.

6. BEING A SAGE

6. BEING A SAGE

Once there was a celibate man who tried to bugger a donkey.
The donkey kicked him in the balls and ran away.

Gone was the donkey. Gone was the celibacy.
The man lost face.

If you say, "Whatever is to happen, happens"
This is what will happen!
Says Tuka, you'll lose either way.

125

For a bedbug the bed is a mountain
So hard to ascend
I can understand how difficult to overcome itself
The human mind must find
After all a worm would always cling
To the core of the tiny fruit that contains it
The beggar picking food from garbage
Imagines himself a king
A frog would cherish its estate of mud
Frowning upon the very concept of an ocean

Says Tuka,
It is the same:
Just see it as it is.
It's a matter of scale.

Said the tiger to the jackal,
"Forgive me, dear fellow, if I eat you.
After all, I'm sure you realize
You are mortal.
Why starve me to death, too?"

The other one replied, "Sir!
Your argument is indeed faultless.
The body is destined to die.
Why not sacrifice your noble self?"

Each one perfectly understood
The other's point of view.
Says Tuka, I know what happens
When tricksters persuade each other.

Some diseases are born of your own body
So will you treat them as your offspring?

Medicinal herbs to treat those diseases
Are found in far-off forests
So will you say they are no remedies?

Says Tuka
The body's relationship with the self
Is a similar nexus.

I wind up the thread
And send my kite into the sky

I have pawned myself
To preserve my selfhood

My debt is secure with interest
Where there is a seed, there is a sprout;
Preserve its capacity to grow.

Says Tuka, I serve with the certainty
That God isn't other than me.

Get nothing to eat
Breed no children
But let Narayana
Bless you

This is what I
Teach myself
This is what I
Preach

Let your body
Go to seed
Let calamities
Fall on you
Let Narayana
Live in your mind

Says Tuka
All this
Is bound
To perish
Remember
Gopal
Your sole
Benefit

129

What awareness creates is here to stay.
It is the light within the light of eternity.

What the mind meets is exquisitely met.
It is never destined to be separated.

Absolute being is not a remembered embrace.
It is housed in one's own awareness.

Says Tuka, don't let the bond of love break:
You will find love wherever you are.

For a thoroughbred, a slight prod is enough;
Flog a common horse, it won't run.

What more can I tell you?
Listen and think about it.

I am not one to argue fiercely,
To physically draw your attention.

Says Tuka, if your face is darkened already,
Why don't you hang your head in shame?

When the sun is reflected in water filled in a jar,
The sun is not wet;
Though fire burns wood, fire itself is not wood—
But something else altogether;
Likewise, Narayana informs every living being,
Yet He is Being Itself, apart from all its forms.
He is the neutral witness of the act of living.

Each human being experiences its own unique destiny
In this world. God paints Himself in a bizarre variety
Of colours. He is like an ascetic
Who has ceased to care about His own form.

One becomes what one chooses to be, in the end.
Thus persons are different from one another.
Good and evil and that grey between them
Determine our own blend of joy and suffering.

Says Tuka, God is a vast jig-saw puzzle of which we are
Mere tiny bits. Grasp Him whole and the pieces all fit.

Whirl around yourself
And the world
Seems to whirl
Around you

Stand still
And everything
Is stilled
Within a vast stillness

Yell
And echoes will ring
Says Tuka—
When clouds race
The moon seems to run

Life is too short for me to read books
And I am no intellectual to grasp their meaning anyway

Whatever I may gain I will gain in Vithoba's name
I shall hold on to what I have already earned

If I try to develop any dialectical skills
Perhaps mere argument will land me in trouble

Says Tuka, I make demands like a child to its parents,
I am sure that the Merciful One will yield

This world is only a camp for us.
We view our body as an object.

Cause and effect is a temporary measure:
With a lightning leap we reach our goal.

We conduct our business as a mere formality:
We are not involved in these transactions.

Says Tuka, our *karma* has been deducted at the source:
We have no profit; we have no loss.

There are no larders in the nests of birds
Narayana bears their burden

A python lies in its own home
And Pandurang looks after it

The *chataka* bird refuses to drink stagnant water
God is the blue cloud that rains for its sake

Says Tuka, we too are creatures like ants
Pandurang takes care of our needs

Is the Sun made more real
By a rooster's crowing?

Then why O Lord do You give me
The burden of being Your devotee?

Would You ever starve
If Your slave stopped You from eating?

Says Tuka,
Ananta holds all the reins of being.

One cannot point to love
One cannot speak of it
One's mind understands
Its own experience

No mother's milk
Feeds a baby tortoise
It grows in its shell
By its mother's grace

Who tells an unborn snake to hide itself
As soon as it emerges from an egg?
A deaf-mute cannot speak but innately
Knows the difference between sweet and salt

Says Tuka, ask your own mind what's good for you
Don't consult those big experts

Don't crush a flower
To possess its fragrance
Don't eat a baby
Because you love it

Don't try to lick
The liquid glow of a pearl
Don't break a musical instrument
To find out its sound

Don't covet the reward
For doing your own duty
Says Tuka O people
I'm telling you a principle

Good for me God
I am a peasant
Or else I'd be
A victim of vanity

You've done the best
You could dear Lord
Tuka dances
Touches your feet

Even a bit
Of knowledge would have
Surely done me
Great harm

I would have lost
The chance to serve saints
I would have got
Robbed instead

I would have been
An arrogant brat
Taking the straight
Road to hell

Says Tuka, the pride
Of greatness becomes
A plunge into
The bottomless pit

These days, poets are found everywhere.
None of them have known real grace.

The prick is lured by flashy language;
He does not give a thought to the difficult part ahead.

Plagiarists! They steal from the work of others
And publish it in their own name.

Says Tuka, if I tell them I know the truth,
They'll just shut their eyes because they won't see it.

By collecting a heap of leftovers,
They lay out their feast of poetry.

Such sinners are doomed to stew in hell,
As long as the sun and the moon are in heaven.

Says Tuka, O poet, worship Narayana alone.
All other pursuits are unreal and disastrous.

Those compelled to wander
Are spent by their walk;
There is only one door
That allows one to enter:

Vithoba's feet
Are the quintessence of life:
Do not ever
Leave them.

He has made life
Accessible to all:
It needs no secret
Teaching to grasp.

Says Tuka, it fulfils
All that you desire:
It has a root and a trunk
And its branches spread vast.

The main message is absolutely clear:
This whole world is God.

First, scatter your own ego to the winds,
Then you will pass the crucial test.

This is the one decisive thing
To know about absolute being.

Says Tuka, once the mind is blown up,
There is neither a cause nor an effect.

God drinks up the temple;
Makes all water dry.
This is neither my personal view
Nor some occult quiz.

See it for yourself:
The trickle becomes the deluge
Flooding rivers and oceans.

The child born to the sterile woman
Wears a single ring in two ears.

Says Tuka, to experience freedom from space
One must taste the flavour of sweetness itself.

It isn't what you do.
It isn't what you think.
It isn't what people are aware of.
It isn't what your heart feels.
It isn't what troubles and tires you.
Nor is it an ill omen.
All these are only words.

It isn't what suddenly besieges you.
Nor is it what runs naked in the streets.
Says Tuka, see it spontaneously:
Spontaneous being
Is always one and the same thing.

He who eats too much
Farts too much
Such wise guys are beyond
Their own control
Arse bared to public view
They glower at the viewers
For noticing

Then there's the one
Who gambles and loses
Complaining about injustice
And the woman who loves to fuck
Who curses her lover for her pregnancy
When she suffers the pangs of child-birth

Says Tuka
Such characters
Injure
Their own humanity

The art of seeking takes different forms:
But cream is churned only to separate the butter.

The empty space between a bird and a fruit
Is never an obstacle for a bird.

Devotion is a full and final settlement:
You get what you pay for and that's it.

Says Tuka I saved bit by bit for a long time
Today I have paid in full.

Sometimes one must let one's life flow like water finding its way.
Sometimes one may lie in a bed of luxury.
Sometimes one has to become what time demands of one.
Sometimes it is a gourmet's feast laid out.
Sometimes stale breadcrumbs for sheer survival.
Sometimes one travels in a comfortable vehicle.
Sometimes one goes barefoot all the way.
Sometimes one gets to wear the choicest garments.
Sometimes one has to wear tattered clothes.
Sometimes one has all the wealth in the world.
Sometimes one has to brave dire straits.
Sometimes one meets saintly people.
Sometimes one has to suffer the company of villains.
Says Tuka: know it well
Joys and sorrows must be equal on one's scale.

Hired mourners also cry
Without tears or feelings

Likewise, devotion to God
Can be mere whitewash

A forced labourer pretends to work hard
Only to run away at the first chance

Says Tuka the spark of a glow-worm
Cannot kindle a flame

Choose the route that reaches
Where you want to go
Do not go by mere hearsay.

Listen to me! Doesn't your inner feeling
Know its way?

No virgin knows what it is
To deliver a child:
There's no alternative to experience.

Says Tuka, remain intent:
The clouds will wither, the Sun will shine.

If one stands up
To argue or fight
One gets into a mess

Reeds don't
Need to exert any force of their own
They accept the force of water

If one tries to be tough
One meets one's match
The humble stay out of trouble

Says Tuka
Blend with all
You'll join
A global family

If you want to make
Love to fire
Don't hesitate
To sleep on a pyre

Once you set
Your heart upon it
It matters little
If you'd burn or live

Nothing'll attack you here
Except fear
A shaky warrior finds
His weapon too heavy to bear

Says Tuka
I cannot be said
To have made up my mind
Unless I had absolute faith

7. BEING A SAINT

Nobody becomes a saint merely by making poems.
Nobody becomes a saint just by being a saint's kin.

A saint is not known by the manner of his dress.
A saint is not known by his family's name.
A saint does not wait for the chance to become a saint.

Nobody becomes a saint just by carrying a begging bowl.
Nobody becomes a saint only by wearing rags.
Nobody becomes a saint by delivering songs and sermons.
Nobody becomes a saint by telling sacred myths.
Nobody becomes a saint by reciting the Vedas.
Nobody becomes a saint by performing rites.

Nobody becomes a saint through penance or pilgrimage.
Nobody becomes a saint by living alone in forests.
Nobody becomes a saint by merely wearing beads.
Nobody becomes a saint by merely smearing ashes.

Says Tuka, all these so-called saints have worldly desires
As long as they do not have one unflinching faith.

Trees, creepers and the creatures of the forest
Are my kith and kin.
And birds that sweetly sing.

This is bliss! How I love being alone!
Here I am beyond good and evil;
Commit no sin.

The sky is my canopy, the earth my throne.
My mind is free to dwell wherever it will.

A piece of cloth, one all-purpose bowl
Take care of all my bodily needs.
The wind tells me the time.

I feast on the cuisine of Hari's lore,
A delighted connoisseur.

Says Tuka, I talk to myself
For argument's sake.

We battle all day
We battle all night
We battle with the world
And with our own mind

We remain alert
For a sudden assault
We have to make
A constant stand

Says Tuka,
The power of Your name
Gives us the strength
To thwart them all

Those who experience
Cosmic Being
Are close to Him
Seeing them
Is to be
Free from sin

They see all things
As equal
Covet nothing
Violate nothing

Says Tuka—
The whole argument
About differences
Ends here.

He who identifies
With the battered and the beaten
Mark him as a saint
For God is with him

The good man's mind
Is soft outside
And soft inside
Say it's like butter

He holds
Every forsaken man
Close to his heart
He treats
A slave
As his own son

Says Tuka
I won't be tired
To repeat again
Such a man
Is God
In person.

A woman out of her mind
Isn't aware
Of her own
Nakedness

One has no regard
For those
Who sham

A mirage
May seem deep
But it's no drink
For the thirsty

The dauntless
Warrior
Doesn't wait
For others
To join
His battle

Says Tuka
The true saint's
Being is
His behaviour

Who says I travelled far and wide
To spread His word?

My father is almighty.
His measure has the sweep of the wind.

Whose reign is this?
He gave me His voice.

Says Tuka, I am sure.
I have no more fear.

People think I am God:
Hell! This is sheer corruption.

Now punish me as You like:
Have my head, You hold the knife.

I have no such right
That they should worship me.

Says Tuka, O my Father, my Mother!
My own mind knows this is sin.

We are lucky! We are lucky!
For a copper vessel, we use a dried gourd.

Others take pride in owning cattle;
We are content with rats and mice.

People ride horses and elephants;
We walk in raw-hide shoes.

Says Tuka, we are barely clothed,
To touch us, even death does not dare.

We slaves of Vishnu
Are softer than wax
We are hard enough
To shatter a thunderbolt

Dead yet alive
Asleep but aware
Ask for anything
We shall give it

We strip ourselves naked
To clothe the needy
We strike down the wicked
Without batting an eyelid

We are more loving
Than natural parents
We are deadlier
Than mortal enemies

We are sweeter than the tonic
Of immortality
And more bitter
Than the deadliest poison

Says Tuka
Ours is a wholesome flavour
As good as anyone
That wishes to savour

Don't kill a snake
Before the eyes of a saint
For the saint's being
Includes all living things
And he's easily
Hurt

A single hair
Plucked from one's body
Causes instant pain
And the soul that perceives
Life as a community
Always suffers

To those who equate
Their being
With everything
Even the other
Is a sensation
Of the self

Says Tuka
I give you
The very root
Of ethics
Be happy to worship
The Lord of All Being
In your own being

The pyre on which
Dead bodies burn
Becomes
By Your grace
Our bed of bliss

Or else
My words
Would be hollow
And they wouldn't
Bear fruit

Bless me
O Lord
That these trees
These shrubs
These stones
Will relate to my blood

Says Tuka
I've staked
The whole of my life
To realize You
O Pandurang
In Your
Entirety

Wherever I go
You go with me
You lead me
Holding my hand

I seem to walk
But You are my prop
You walk with me
Make my burdens light

Whatever I blurt
You make it sound right
I hesitate no more
You've made me bold

To me every man
Is mankind's guardian
All are my darling
Soulmates

Says Tuka
I live as I please
Within me is bliss
And peace outside

A benefactor is only he
Who reminds you of Narayana

The rest of mortals
Cannot relieve you of your misery

Cry only for their help
Who can show you the way out

Says Tuka be grateful only to him
Who has transcended his own being

The more these people admire me
The more I am ashamed of myself
For I know there is nothing in me to be admired.

Like a measure used over and over
i am worn out now
This wasn't for any personal gain.

I am like a tender thorn with a piercing point
I am hollow inside and easy to break
I am like a painted tint that looks perfect
But being lifeless is a pale likeness of real life.

Says Tuka O Lord I am all wasted
Without experiencing You.

VERSES COMPOSED WHEN TUKARAM'S MANUSCRIPTS IN THE INDRAYANI RIVER WERE RECOVERED UNDAMAGED AFTER THIRTEEN DAYS

Today it is thirteen days since I began to fast not even drinking water
And yet O my Almighty Parent, You have not emerged

O Lord of the Senses what is wrong with You?
Why do You cover Yourself with stone?
I will sacrifice my life at Your altar now
Pandurang, I'll kill myself:
O Vithabai, my Mother, I had hoped so much!
Now my being is all I can destroy, Pandurang.

Says Tuka, I am about to leave now,
I shall give up my life unto You.

I have been terribly unjust:
I tried the limit of your forgiveness.
Just because people instigated me,
I allowed my mind to be ravaged by fury.

You have relieved me of all that tremendous stress.
How despicable I am, how unchaste indeed!
I kept my eyes shut
For full thirteen days.

I made you bear the entire burden of my being.
I made you suffer my thirsting and my starving
I made you sustain my life itself.

You kept my manuscripts safe under water.
You saved me from being damned by the public.
Says Tuka, truly, you lived up to your name.

No blade was about to fall on my head
Nor was I going to be stabbed in the back;
Yet I howled so much, O Hari! as though it was the very end.

You divided yourself equally on either side:
You were with me and deep inside the river, too.
In neither place did you allow
The tiniest trace of damage to be done.

For much smaller crimes,
Real parents would kill their own children.
What you have forgiven was
An offence only you could bear with.

Says Tuka, O Merciful One!
There is none more generous than you.
What more can I say?
I have become speechless.

Let anyone cut my throat;
Let wicked people torture me as they please:
Never again will I do
Anything that might strain you.

I have committed this beastly blunder once:
To force you to stand in the river
And protect my notebooks.

I did not pause to think
What right I had to ask your help,
Why the Almighty One should bear my burden.

What has happened has happened.
It is useless to talk about it now.
But henceforth, says Tuka,
One will have to watch oneself.

You are kind as a mother;
You shelter the poor like us;
Unannounced you came to me
In the form of a baby.

You brought me peace,
In a chubby form that I could touch and feel.
You threw your arms around me
And calmed my mind.

You showed me mercy in the form of people.
You gave me blessings at the hands of the saints.
You made my mind innocent
Of the nature of sorrow.

Says Tuka, I have been so unfair.
Forgive me, O my mother.
Will I ever put you to trouble
For my sake, again?

I am a poor creature.
How can I fathom your depth
O Pandurang ?
Once you are determined
Nothing is impossible for you to do.

I had no patience before.
I am a moron and of mean morals.
But your mercy is so vast
You did not turn me down.

You are the God of gods.
You are the soul of the cosmos.
Why did a small slave like me
Have to beg your mercy?

Says Tuka, O Cosmic One,
I am really a sinner:
And to compound my sin further
I made a demonstration at your door.

You are gentler than a mother
You are cooler than the moon
You are finer than water
O ripples of pure love

What simile can I use for you?
O Perfect Man
You compare with
Yourself alone.
All names are worth
Being sacrificed to you.

You created the drink
That prevents death:
Yet your own flavour
Is more exquisite.
You generated
The Five Elements.
You are the Lord
Of all being.
I shall say nothing now—
Just lay my head upon your feet.
Says Tuka, O Lord of Pandhari,
Forgive all my sins.

I am wicked;
I am unjust:
I can repeat it
Again and again.
O Vitthal!
Let me remain
At your feet.
No more; no more
Life in this world
For me.
The pull of *karma*
Would never let
My mind stay still.
Thought is too vibrant;
Its spectrum is unstable:
And its colours snare me
Into precarious illusions.
Says Tuka, cut off
The cord of my anxiety now,
O Lord of Pandhari!
Settle in my heart.

8. BEING BLESSED

Tukaram Describes his Mystic Initiation

My great good Guru gave me a blessing
But I was not able to serve him at all

I was on my way to the river for a dip
Suddenly he found me and placed his hand on my head

He asked for half-a-pound of clarified butter for food
But in that dreamlike state I forgot all about it

Perhaps he sensed that I was going astray
Therefore he came in such a hurry to initiate me

He gave me a clue to my spiritual lineage
By naming Raghav Chaitanya and Keshav Chaitanya

He said his own name was Babaji
And gave me the mantra: "Rama Krishna Hari."

It was the tenth day of the bright fortnight of Magha
And a Thursday, the Day of the Guru, when he embraced me,
says Tuka

Placing his hand over my four-fold body
He revealed to me the mind-blown state of being

He stamped upon me that mind-blown state of being
It gathered into an absolute blue luminosity

Red, white, yellow, blue, and black
Colours rippled out in various ways

The self shed all colours to enter the realm
Of its own pure and luminous transparence

No image can convey that luminosity
Its absolute formless stillness

Where to arrive from? Where to depart for?
One must only remain in such pure continuity

Continuity means being without break
It is more absolute than all that can be

To describe it is to break its pure integrity
How can one describe in words the absoluteness of being?

Says Tuka, whereof all language must remain silent,
Thereof what can one say? Babaji revealed it to me

In fifteen days I realized God:
I found Vithoba Who has no form.

I settled on the Bhambgiri hill
And set my mind on the Being beyond being.

Knowing this was Nirvana, I sat down in the proper posture,
Began to meditate on the Lord.

Snakes, scorpions, tigers attacked me:
I was assaulted from all sides.

Just as camphor vapourizes into a flame,
Says Tuka, my body became.

In the pool of bliss,
Bliss is all ripples.
Bliss is the body
Of bliss.

How can I describe it?
It's too embarassing.
There's no will left.
It compels more and more.

When the mother craves,
It's the unborn's fancy.
What grows inside
Is reflected out.

Says Tuka,
What I pour out
Into this mould
Is the face of my innermost
Experience.

Bliss soured to become the cream of bliss.
Blessed, I've begun to churn the cream.

My body rocks and sways in bliss.
My arms are lost, my eyes are lost.

Look! How Narayana gathers up Himself!
Look! How he transforms His properties!

Says Tuka, He is reaching the brim now!
In an instant, He is going to overflow!

Water has turned
Into the sky.
One has lapsed
Into all.

How to contain it now?
It ripples in itself.

What can spill out of it?
It has closed up itself.

Says Tuka,
This is
The end of the world
Sunrise is sunset.

I've got addicted
To it.
I am tight
With arousal.

"She's crazy for God!
She's crazy for God!"
Says the world
Of me.

I made love
So secretly.
But it's come out.
It can't be hid.

Says Tuka,
Having met Him,
One is cut off
From all else.

174

The body has become
Too intense.
One's own colour
Is fused with His.

One is fixed
Within Him.
It's like root
And sprout.

Falling
Into the ocean,
Where can a droplet
Choose to go?

Tuka says,
This is nothing new.
God knows.

The mind is settled.
The breath crippled.
The last symptom
Has shown up.

Half-closed,
The eyes glow.
The throat chokes.
Hair stand on ends.

Awareness is
Awed by itself.
I am too happy
To get out of me.

It is the dawn
Of the luminous blue.
I am drunk
With immortality.

The Sun and the Moon
Orbit the soul.
Ecstasy contracts
Into ecstasy.

Says Tuka, in love
I gently
Rock away
It's a sure dissolve.

I cannot even shit in peace, my Lord!
The smallest movement cuts off my contact with you.

You appear to be so irrepressible!
And why should I ever put a stop to these visions?

Even when I have no company
Your colours make me babble.

Says Tuka, O God,
I cannot yet begin to serve you.

There is a whole tree within a seed
And a seed at the end of each tree
That is how it is between you and me
One contains the Other.
There is a ripple on water
That is itself water.
Says Tuka, the image
Merges with the mirror.

Worldly life has every vice
We are cured by singing His praise

Heaven, Earth and Hell are cleansed
There is no trace of inequity

From now on it's a zone of bliss
That has no end and we are pure

Says Tuka we live in the only One
Alone in bliss savouring bliss

9. ABSOLUTELY BEING

I came out
Of my own womb

My prayers answered
My longing vanished

Now I am truly strong
It's long since I died

Looking both ways
Tuka is just as he is

I'm nothing
A nobody
Native
Of nowhere
I am alone
In my own place

I do not visit
Any place
I neither come
Nor go
I talk
To emptiness

Nobody
Belongs to me
I belong
To nobody
None of this
Is true

I do not
Have to live
I do not
Have to die
I am
Undivided

Says Tuka
I have no name
Or form
I am neither active
Nor passive

I have seen my death with my own eyes
O what an incomparable festival it was

All the three worlds were filled with ecstasy
I experienced it becoming the cosmic being

I was confined to the sole territory of my ego
Having renounced it, I enjoy the abundance of it all

I do not mourn the facts of birth and death now
I leave the remains of my shrunken self here

Narayana has given me refuge
All my feelings lie at His feet

Says Tuka, the whole world is His imprint
And I wear it like a tattoo on my body

Too scarce to occupy an atom,
Tuka is vast as the sky.

I swallowed my death, gave up the corpse,
I gave up the world of fantasy.

I have dissolved God, the self, and the world
To become one luminous being.

Says Tuka, now I remain here
Only to oblige.

The world has become a form of light.
Darkness is gone.

There is no place to hide here.
Everything is explicitly spread.

The day of truth has dawned.
Everything is larger than language.

Says Tuka, only for the sake of life,
One is still clinging to the dividing line.

A stick in his hand
Tuka chases his own corpse

He takes it to the crematorium
Where bodies are laid to burn

He punishes it
For its past deeds

He fears nothing
For God can take all pleasure and pain

This is why I am determined
To make such a clean exit

Says Tuka, it is healthier to die
Than to have a body to be punished

I staked everything
On my last day being sweet

Now I am certainly at peace
I have stopped thirsting after it

I am happy now that I spent myself
Singing His sacred name

Says Tuka, I am married to salvation
I'll spend a few days playfully with my bride

I speak a language of silence.
I am already dead.

Being for me is not being among people.

What I consume is already sacrificed.
I am alone in the company of all.
I have cut off all connections
Between ends and means.

Says Tuka, I am not what I seem to be:
If you have any questions, ask Pandurang.

Tuka has descended into Tuka:
Heaven, Earth, Hell watch in wonder.

My only performance of penance
Is my singing of His praises.

Tuka sits in heaven's vehicle
As all the saints bear witness.

God starves after pure devotion
So much, He lifts Tuka to heaven!

Hari's name my sail I cross
The ocean of apparent life

Surrender my self to all these saints
And I am so free so free

Hari's name my sword my horse
I smash the chariot of worldly life

Hari's name my bow and arrow
Death flees from its battle with me

I rule the earth, the nether world
And heaven too in Hari's name

Says Tuka I have truly become
The right hand of Vitthal

The word is not confined
To one country.

It does not hit one person
Or miss another.

My language is of
Cosmic being.

One who carries the quiver
Just shoots His arrows.

Says Tuka, it is not I who aim:
God hits you.

187

The night has passed.
What's sleep? I haven't seen it.

I have built my nest in Narayana.
My joy does not cease.

I have compressed my space.
I have no room for myself.

Says Tuka, we are contained together.
We do not split for one moment.

I went beyond modesty
To attain my goal.

I entered the ocean of worldly experience
To emerge dancing at the other shore.

I tied my own to the Lord's name
To make it a most pleasurable game.

Says Tuka, what reaches people is
The call of my residual speech.

We have built ourselves a house in empty space
We reside in formless eternity

We are one with a reality bereft of illusions
We experience a wholeness that cannot be fragmented

Says Tuka, we do not have an ego any more,
We have become what is immutable and pure

I burnt the seed itself
And pop it went
Now I have gone beyond
Life and death

What space can enclose my form?
My body itself is God.

Sugar does not become
Sugarcane again.
We will never grow
In another womb.

Says Tuka,
This is absolute awakening:
There is Pandurang
In every thing.

The absolutely naked
Use their hands for a cup

When one really needs God
The mind presents Him

The alms one gets fulfil one's wishes
One sleeps in open spaces

Tuka is clothed by the sky itself
He lives beyond all perception

All time and space have become auspicious:
To think of the inauspicious is inauspicious.

The light one holds has removed the night:
One does not even know what night is.

Pleasure is no different from pain.
Even strokes of misfortune will bring gain.

Says Tuka, every living thing
Is now my blessing.

For me God is dead.
Let him be for those who need him.

I shall speak of him no more.
I shall not name him again.

We have slain each other.

In his praise, I cursed him.
Lord, what an endless affair!

Says Tuka, I have squandered my whole life after him.
Now I would like to sit still.

My mortality is finished.
I am deathless.
The home is erased.
The base is wiped out.
The hollow body has been emptied.

There was a deluge
And it is over.
I continue to exist
By sheer will.

Says Tuka, what I inherited
Is what I celebrate.

Mankind for us has become wilderness;
In the name of Vitthal it is the same.

Wherever I see, I find my parents:
There is Vitthal, there is Rakhumai.

The forest and the city are identical:
There are no divisions in my kind of space.

I do not remember joy; I do not remember sorrow.
Tuka dances in absolute wonder.

I shall sing of Him forever.
I shall raise His slogan forever.
I shall go on telling the story of Hari forever.
For that's what pleases me.

I wear the jewels of pure joy.
I rock to the ecstatic beat of freedom.

I do not even know if I am.
I have a body that I don't feel I have.

Says Tuka, I have become a form of fire:
Good and evil cannot enter me.

I was so thirsty
I drank up my thirst
I was so hungry
I ate my hunger

My very self
Became nothing
Vitthal
Found me clean

There was no room
For desire
The mind collapsed
At His feet

What remained
Was still Tuka
His life was lost
To itself

Flesh, skin, bone
God savours all

Those who take on Hari's hue
Leave behind no residue

Shankha, the demon, swallowed the Vedas
He is now the conch-shell of God

Says Tuka, such a greedy one is He
To consume *Bhakti*.

194

Tuka got up and went home
Leaving God alone in his temple

The slave marvelled how his Lord was at peace
Now that everything was as ordered

Once Hari has stretched Himself
On His serpent-bed of infinity
Nothing remains to be done
By His devotee

Asking everybody to go home
Tuka himself left, too
He told the people,
"God is asleep."

Because I cannot search
I hold on to His feet.

"Now," I beg, "Narayana,
Take me out of people's sight."

My mind returns to its source
To vanish altogether.

Tuka has lost all memory
He speaks he walks but silently.

To speak only "Vitthal", to see only Vitthal,
To make Vitthal my life and soul,

My mind has gone to Him, never to return,
Vitthal its only goal.

I have untied the knot where it was fastened the hardest;
I am free to embrace Him as long as I wish:

Says Tuka, there's no room for desire and rage in me,
My entire body is filled with Vitthal

I feel like dancing
The beat comes from you

Like a puppet on a string
You make me swing

Tinted by Your name and form
My senses come alive

Says Tuka, Pandurang
Envelops me

The power of rapturous singing
Is just out of this world.

You have given it as a gift to me, O Lord.
Let me serve You without interruption.

The tide of love that swells in my body,
Never ebbs, but sweeps ever higher.

Says Tuka, I unearth Your immortal name
With my voice.

Between you and me there is no difference
I am simply making fun

You are exactly my shape and size
You stretch me as you will

I am really inside you
You serve yourself out of me

Inside you I stay very still
Inside me is your strong will

With my mouth, it is you who speak;
Inside you, I just stay cool

Says Tuka, O God
Our names get so mixed up

I was lonely in nothingness
I had no companion

See now? How this Lord of the Senses
Makes me go crazy?

He hides His own body in mine
To give me company

Says Tuka, I never knew
That my own feeling would destroy me

I have no work.
See, how empty I am.
I do whatever that catches my fancy.
I am a motionless visionary.
My odd obsession
Makes the whole world writhe in laughter.
All of a sudden, Tuka is cut
Away from the world.

The real reason why you created this drama and its actors
Is simply your love of theatre.

Otherwise, even I have long since suspected
That the tiger and the cow are both wooden puppets.

The play as a whole makes only one sense
That nothing is divisible: one light is many flames.

There's more good news, says Tuka,
The mirror is empty.

10. A FAREWELL TO BEING

Born a *shudra*, I have been a trader,
This deity comes to me like a sacred heirloom.

I am unable to say any more, but O saints,
I shall honour my pledge to answer your question

I was extremely miserable as a householder
Ever since both my parents died.

Famine reduced me to penury, I lost my honour.
I had to watch one of my wives starve to death.

Ashamed of myself, I suffered great anguish
To find my business in ruins.

The shrine of my deity had fallen apart
And I felt like restoring it first.

In the beginning, I used to perform *keertan* there.
On the day of *ekadashi*, in my untutored way.

I had learnt some sayings of the saints by rote
And I reproduced those with reverence and faith.

I would join the chorus that followed the lead singers,
I would sing the refrain with a pure heart.

I was never ashamed of following the saints.
The dust of their feet was sacred to me.

I worked hard so that my body could endure more.
I helped others as much as I could.

I was so weary of the ways of this world
That I spurned all advice given by my friends.

I made my own mind the sole judge of truth
Rejecting the popular view of life.

I followed the guidance that my Guru gave me in a dream
I held fast to the name of God.

After a while, I was inspired to write poetry
As my mind grasped Vithoba's feet.

I was denounced and assailed some time later
And it hurt my mind.

So I drowned all my manuscripts, appealing to God
To restore them if I was true, and Narayana satisfied me.

If I went into all those details
It would take too long; so I stop here.

Now I am exactly what I seem to you all.
God alone knows what the future is going to be.

I have understood one thing: that Narayana
Never lets down his devotees.

Says Tuka, my only assets in this world are
The poems that Pandurang made me speak.

Tukaram says Farewell to his Colleagues

See me off and go home now,
All of you.

May you attain the good by doing your duty righteously.
My blessings go with you.

You raised me and handed me over to the One.
Now everything will work out for me.

I have followed what I cherished:
It is time to go with the Lord of my breath.

Do not let your affection linger any longer:
Still your troubled minds.

Those who ever joined hands with me
Have achieved man's cherished integrity.

Says Tuka, this is our last meeting:
All I leave behind is stories about me.

We go back to our native place.
Good-bye, God bless you.

This was our only meeting.
We won't be born again.

I beg your forgiveness now
I touch your feet as my last tribute.

Whenever someone reaches home,
Meets the end: say, "Vitthal! Vitthal!"

Say, "Rama Krishna! Rama Krishna!"
Tuka is leaving for Vaikunth.

NOTES AND GLOSSARY

Abhang:
    literally,
        1. absolute; eternal, immutable, ceaseless, unbroken; impeccable, etc.
        2. immortal, primordial; another name for *Brahman*; inviolable, etc.
        3. a Marathi metre; also, any metrical composition in this metre.

the *abhang* is the favourite metre of all *Varkari* poets since the thirteenth century and unlike classical Sanskrit-based metres it is native to Marathi speech and its colloquial forms. It is extremely flexible. It consists of four lines and each line contains three to eight syllables. It has a fluid symmetry maintained by internal or end-rhymes and is often designed to be sung. It originates most probably in oral folk-poetry. Poets such as Jananadev, Namdeo, and Tukaram have given it a classic status in Marathi poetry. Most of Tukaram's compositions are in this metre and even when they are not, in exceptional cases, the term *abhang* is popularly used for practically all of Tukaram's metrical compositions.

Avataras, (the ten)
    "the Fish, the Tortoise, the Boar, the Man-Lion, the Dwarf Man, Parashu Rama, Rama, Krishna, the Buddha, and Kalki are the Ten *Avataras*" according to a verse in the Geeta. These, in the same order, are the incarnations (*avataras*) of Vishnu.

Ananta:
    literally,
        1. endless, infinite, boundless, etc.
        2. name of Vishnu.
        3. name of Shesha, the serpent upon whom Vishnu sleeps.
        4. the sky; space, etc.
        5. used for time, eternity, etc.
        6. used for *Brahman*, or absolute and infinite being; infinity in any sense.

Tukaram uses Ananta as both a name and an attribute of Vitthal who, to the *Varkaris*, is synonymous with Vishnu and Narayana, both of whom are known by many other names. Since each of these names has a unique significance, Tukaram often uses a specific name in a specific context, literally, metaphorically, or suggestively.

Bahinabai Sioorkar :

(1629–1700) is remarkable among the Marathi poet-saints not just because she is a woman; so were Muktabai and Janabai long before her; Bahinabai is unique because she was an orthodox, married Brahmin and yet was attracted to *Bhakti* and particularly to the poetry of Tukaram about whom she heard in distant Kolhapur from a *keertan*-performer called Jayaramaswami; she was obsessed by the idea of meeting Tukaram in person and dreamt that Tukaram blessed her and became her guru; this resulted in her husband beating her up in jealous fury; he was horrified that his wife, a Brahmin, should want to make a Shudra who had no scriptural knowledge her guru; however, the husband changed his mind when persuaded by another Brahmin and accompanied Bahinabai to Dehu; there they saw Tukaram and attended his *keertans*; Bahinabai's vivid account of Dehu and Tukaram are like a poetic journal that vividly recreates scenes in evocative detail; this is the only contemporary eyewitness account of Tukaram available to us; Bahinabai's autobiography and verses are translated into English prose by Justin E.Abbott and have been recently republished with a perceptive foreword by Anne Feldhaus.

Bhagawadgeeta:

often also referred to in the abbreviated form "the Geeta"; "The Song of the Lord" depicting the celebrated dialogue between Arjuna and Krishna during the *Mahabharata* war and a section of the *Bheeshmaparva*, a chapter of the Hindu epic, *Mahabharata*; regarded by many Hindus as the essence of all scriptures and the revelation by Lord Vishnu of his own nature and cosmic role that explains *karma*, man's duty in this world and the laws that govern his behaviour, the design of human destiny, and the divine, cyclic design by which Vishnu Himself assumes different *avataras* or incarnations in the human world to remove the specific form of evil that afflicts each Age or Epoch; this is also seen as a dialogue between the individual human ego and the Divine Self or the Whole Being of which the human individual is only a part;

208

Jnanadev produced the first poetic transcreation of the *Bhagawadgeeta* in Marathi in the thirteenth century; these acts of translation into the language of the masses must have been viewed by the Brahmin orthodoxy as acts of heresy.

Bhakta:

literally means a worshipper, a devotee, a votary, an adorer, etc.; it is useful to remember that the original Sanskrit word also means: 1. (a share) allotted, distributed, assigned; as such a *Bhakta* is given "his lot" or "his share of the Divine"; 2. divided; applied to a *Bhakta*, this may assume a spiritual significance; 3. served, worshipped; 4. engaged in, attentive to; 5. attached or devoted to; loyal, faithful.

Bhakti:

devotion, loyalty, faithfulness; engagement, commitment; dedication; reverence, service, homage; the condition of the whole being of a *Bhakta* whose mind and body are totally absorbed in the object of his worship and remain continually directed or oriented towards it; the object of such worship can be an anthropomorphic deity, a symbol, a name, an image, a concept, an abstraction, or the non-discursive or inconceivable "Whole Being" itself.

Bhakti-Marga:

derives from the above; literally, "the way of devotion" or "devotion as the path by which God is realized (by individuals or by a community of devotees)". In reading Tukaram, *Bhakti* should be usually read as the *Bhakti* of Vishnu by any of his one thousand names that are also his epithets but specifically in the form of Vitthal, or Vithoba; see *Varkari*, Vitthal, Pandharpur, "the Brick", etc.

Bhakti Rasa:

would literally mean "the juice of *Bhakti*" or "(the uninterrupted flow of) the feeling of devotion"; "*rasa*" in classical Sanskrit poetics is active feeling, emotion, something akin to "juice" in a physiological sense, thus a somatic action or effect; but the poetics itself is diversely linked and interpreted in terms of religious esotericism, *yoga*, and mysticism; the cryptic precept, "*Raso vai sah*" means, "He is the very *rasa*" which, loosened by paraphrase would mean "God or the Whole Being is Himself that spontaneous flowing juice"; one is making this slight digression because the pioneer Marathi poet-saint Jnanadev was an initiate in the Kashmir Shaiva tradition, the same school of thought to which the great mystic philosopher and poetician, Abhinavagupta belonged; Jnanadev was a *yogi* of the Natha Sect; how he came to worship the deity Vithoba, seen as a form of Vishnu, and became a founder of the *Varkari Bhakti* movement is a perennial mystery; but the *"rasa"* or "feeling" part of *Bhakti*, the sensuous and palpable form of worshipping God as a devotee, focused on a specific image and a "name", begins with Jnanadev and his contemporaries; poetry and music, singing songs and chanting, were believed to produce a distinct *"rasa"* or "flow of feeling", of oneness with God; this is the *"rasa"* or "state of being in a continuous flow" that makes *Varkaris* sing, dance, chant the name of God, and create that "total theatre" where everybody is a part of the grand performance of worship; the pilgrimage to Pandharpur and the festival of Vithoba there have to be witnessed to get an idea of how *"Bhakti-rasa"* a distinct universe of feeling, envelops the *"Bhaktas"* with a sense of communion; Tukaram's poetry is described as a poetry of *"Bhakti-rasa"* which includes a wide range of emotions and different personae depicting the devotee's many-faceted relationship with God; it is useful to bear this in mind because the *Varakari Bhakta* may be viewing Tukaram's poetry as the poetry of *Bhakti-rasa*, which is not quite the same feeling that we experience ourselves in our normal life and assume that others experience; nor do we associate such a feeling with poetry and its impact.

Brahma:

the "Creator"; one of the gods in the Hindu pantheon; he is depicted in the *Puranas* as having sprung from a lotus rising out of the navel of Vishnu.

Brahman:

original Sanskrit form of the word which is *Brahma* in Marathi; neuter gender; often translated as "the Supreme Being" etc., and variously interpreted by Vedantic philosophers and commentators; it is at once the primordial as well as the ultimate condition of being, a concept of "being-in-itself" which is beyond determination, definition or description. As such, it is a paradoxical concept of the inconceivable, which is the source of all phenomena and all possible concepts thereof. It is used in the sense of "autonomous self" or "the principle of spontaneous creation, existence, and dissolution". In mystical thought, *"Brahman"* can be experienced as "bliss" or "beatitude" or "a sense of boundless being". It is "ecstasy" in terms of its outward signs and "enstasy" in terms of "self- contained sense of bliss". During the last decade of his life, Tukaram unexpectedly met Babaji, a liberated *yogi*, who initiated him into an experience of such "beatitude". Tukaram's evolution from being a *Bhakta* to becoming a mystic is clearly seen in his poems. There was never a contradiction between his worship of Vithoba and his yearning to experience beatitude or "oneness with All Being". There are people, in fact, who believe that Tukaram's body simply disintegrated and returned to the state of absolute, unconditioned being, leaving no trace of its material form and identity. I have no comment to offer on this except that if true, it would be real poetic justice.

Brahmin:
the highest among the castes; considered pure and chaste; the "twice-born" priestly caste that has a privileged access to the scriptures and the sole right to recite, teach, and interpret them; they conduct religious ceremonies, perform rites, and adjudicate matters and disputes concerning *dharma* of all Hindus; in Tukaram's time, Brahmins in Maharashtra considered all the other castes as either "non-caste" or "outside the sacred circle" or as Shudras: causing pollution in varying degrees; Tukaram describes himself as a Shudra and a Yatiheen, which means Jatiheen, or low-born, and pointedly mentions that the Brahmins would not even concede him the right to read and write, let alone discuss spiritual matters; he also attacks depravity among Brahmins and holds them responsible for corruption of religion as well as ethics in personal and social life; Tukaram propounds that anyone who is pure in spirit is a true Brahmin and accidents of birth have nothing to do with it; in Tukaram's view any individual who is God-oriented or tuned to "the Whole Being" is a Brahmin or the *Brahman*-oriented person, because "caste" is a quality of mind determined by purity of awareness rather than by any physical or material property or criterion.

Brick, the:
this has been used as a proper noun because it refers to "the Brick" on which the image of Vitthal at Pandharpur stands and is an

integral part of the iconography of Vitthal; the Marathi word for brick is "*veet*", and some folk-etymologists would derive the word Vitthal itself from it; the mythological significance of "the Brick" is the following story: Pundalik, a resident of Pandharpur and a devotee of Vishnu/Vitthal was visited by God Himself, who had heard of Pundalik's total dedication; Pundalik was so absorbed in his own work that he threw a brick that was handy in the direction of his divine visitor, asking him to stand; after that, Pundalik forgot all about God whom he had kept waiting, while he remained absorbed in his own work; God would not leave without Pundalik's permission; he has remained standing on the brick ever since; twenty-eight eons are said to have elapsed since Pundalik asked God to wait on the brick; this is how God is found in Pandharpur where his devotees can visit Him; "the Brick" may mean Vitthal Himself in Tukaram's poetry; Tukaram worships Vitthal's feet, which are placed on "the Brick", in humility; because God stands on it, "the Brick" itself is sacred; "the Brick" is also the "base" or "foundation" of God in this world, and as such it is a symbol of *Bhakti* itself, which is the foundation of the Whole Being or *Brahman* for the *Bhakta*; "the Brick" is also a symbol of God's patient, obedient, and respectful attitude towards a true *Bhakta*, epitomized by the story of Pundalik; the *Varkari Bhakta*-poets consider Pundalik as the arch-*Bhakta* and founder of the sacred site and image at Pandharpur.

Chandal:
another term designating a low-caste, a Shudra; originally, a mixed caste of illegitimate progeny of Shudra male and Brahmin female parents; as such, bastards born of prohibited intercaste liasons; a derogatory term used for the lowest born, for the unscrupulous, the sinful, the wicked, the corrupt, and the criminal-minded.

Colour:
the colour of Vishnu is dark blue, the colour of the sky itself, which is the colour of his *avatara*, Krishna; Krishna literally means "the dark one" or even "the black one"; sometimes, in poetry, the colour of Krishna is compared to "a dark blue rain cloud", a monsoonal association with its evocative effect on the Indian mind and its pastoral significance for herdsmen; Krishna was a herdsman, too; the colour of the image of Vitthal is black; the *dhotar* or loin-garment of Vitthal is yellow silk; the name Pandurang, used for

Vithoba or Vitthal was first used in 1270 according to Deleury: its origin is obscure; but Pandurang is close to the Sanskrit word *"pandura"*, which means "yellowish-white" or "fawn-coloured"; in both Sanskrit and Marathi, *"anga"* means body.

Another significance of colour needs to be pointed out in the context of Tukaram's visual imagery, especially when he is describing his experience of beatitude: when Tukaram meditates on Vitthal's form, the image becomes a formless expanse of luminous blue that turns into an intense incandescence; but when he describes the effect of his initiation into the state of beatitude induced by his Guru Babaji, Tukaram describes a state of ecstasy in which he begins to see luminous ripples in five colours: red, yellow, blue, white, and black: these colours vibrate, pulsate, and keep changing from one into the other in a rhythmic manner.

One more thing to remember is that in Marathi the verb *"rangane"* which means "to be coloured" also refers to the experience of being absorbed in any activity in such a way that one's very appearance is "coloured" by it; this applies to devotion, worship, the act of singing and dancing, the act of chanting the names of God, and in Tukaram's case, the act of creating poetry or "speaking" in that special sense; in all these, "one is coloured by what one thinks of and does" or "one's very being is coloured by one's awareness"; any performance that becomes increasingly exciting or absorbing is described in Marathi, literally, as something "that is becoming more and more colourful" or "is gaining colour"; "getting coloured by *Bhakti- rasa*" is another typical expression.

Dehu:

Tukaram's native village; this is situated on the banks of the river Indrayani; it is part of the earliest or one of the earliest-known agricultural belts in Maharashtra, it is accessible by rail from Bombay or Pune via the Dehu Road Railway Station; by road, it is just an hour's drive from Pune; Tukaram's ancestral house with its shrine is still here and his descendants live there; it also has another temple of Vithoba and several smaller shrines; "the pool" in the river Indrayani where Tukaram's manuscripts were sunk and then miraculously restored is one of the landmarks; another landmark is the place at which Vishnu's chariot of light is believed to have descended to lift Tukaram bodily off to heaven; Dehu, along with Pandharpur and Alandi, is one of the three sacred places *Varkari* pilgrims regularly visit; the Bhamachandra hill,

where Tukaram meditated for fifteen days and received enlightenment, is also near Dehu and so is the Bhandara Hill where
Tukaram wrote his poems; the landscape and the people Tukaram
has described belong to Dehu, which still retains recognizable
traces of its features as they must have been in Tukaram's time.

Deva:
  also "*dev*" in Marathi; God; also god or gods; Tukaram employs
  this word in different senses; often, it is a form of address to the
  image of Vitthal, but to Tukaram Vitthal not only contains the
  specific form in which Vishnu visited Pandharpur and stood on
  "the Brick" at Pundalik's instance but also Vishnu in all his
  avataras, including that of the Buddha to whom Tukaram makes a
  reference in a poem not translated here; the mythology of Vishnu
  and the lore of Krishna are both included in Tukaram's frame of
  reference; but Tukaram's God is also the Supreme Being in a
  monotheistic sense, the Creator and the Ruler, not dissimilar from
  the Judaeo-Christian-Islamic "Father"; but Tukaram uses all three
  genders for God; at the highest level, he conceives God as a form
  of total being, the Whole Being or the Cosmic Self of which the
  human individual is a part; Tukaram's mysticism had both native
  Marathi and traditional Hindu origins but it was also influenced
  by Sufi thought, and Buddhism; the traces of these influences are
  subtly diffused over his work; one has found an existentialist
  current in Tukaram's thought that is constant and growing; though
  he obviously began as a simple devotee, he evolved into a
  monotheistic mystic, and finally into a mystic who went beyond
  theism itself; in some poems, Tukaram has described his whole
  relationship with God as a game of "make-believe" or as "play-ac-
  ting", assigning roles that are mutually reversible. In each poem,
  God has a specific image and role; there are no fixed rules or
  definitions that Tukaram follows; it is worth bearing in mind that
  in many poems, Tukaram sees himself as an irreverent atheist or
  as one making fun of an anthropomorphic idea of God.

Ekadashi:
  literally, "the eleventh (day)"; Maharashtra follows the Hindu
  lunar calendar in which one half of the month is the part of the
  waxing moon and the other is the phase of the waning moon; thus
  the month is divided into "the bright fortnight" and "the dark
  fortnight"; Ekadashi is the eleventh day of the bright fortnight of

the month; the *Varkaris* regard this as Vitthal's day, and fast on it; the Ekadashi days in the months of Ashadha and Kartika are the days of the festival of Vitthal in Pandharpur and a *Varkari* has to make a pilgrimage to the sacred city on these days; of the two, Ashadhi Ekadashi is the bigger festival; hundreds of thousands of Varkaris march to Pandharpur from all over Maharashtra to take part in the festival; many of them carry their own *tumba*-like string instruments and cymbals made of brass, and *chiplyas* or *veenas*; singing and dancing all the way to Pandharpur; they chant *bhajans* or witness *keertan* performances and play games or perform dances which are all "enactments of devotion"; this is a form of a "total theatre" in a ritual event in which everybody participates and the poetry of saints is sung from memory as a part of the performance; Ekadashi, even in months other than Ashadha and Kartika, is a holy day; Tukaram refers to his own performance of *keertan* on every Ekadashi in his own shrine of Vitthal in Dehu; he also makes a pointed reference in another poem to his fasting and keeping awake when he was facing a total financial disaster after the famine, thus serving Vitthal even in times of personal adversity.

Eknath:

was born in 1533 and died in 1599; he lived in Paithan; he is one of the "Great Quartet" of Vithoba's Poets—Jnanadev, Namdeo, Eknath and Tukaram; to paraphrase Bahinabai, a younger poetess and contemporary of Tukaram, the temple of the *Varkari Bhakti* movement was founded by Jnanadev, its walls were built by Namdeo, Eknath built its pillars, and Tukaram was its spire; a prolific poet, Eknath produced work in many genres; he also produced a carefully researched and corrected edition of the *Jnaneshwari*.

Garuda:

"the devourer", "the bird of fire", or "the bird of the sun"; Vishnu's vehicle; this could be the "chariot of fire" or "chariot of light" in which Vishnu carried Tukaram away to Vaikuntha, his heavenly residence, according to the *Varkari* tradition.

Gopala:

"cow-raiser" or "cow-protector", a name of Krishna used for Vitthal by Tukaram in many poems; the name is also used for Krishna's boyhood playmates who were herdsmen like him;

215

Gopala is thus God, the cowherd and his *Bhaktas*, His fellow-cowherds; the "cows" also signify the five senses and "the cowherd" the self that protects them; likewise, the "cows" are the milkmaids or "*gopis*" with whom Krishna flirted and had clandestine affairs; Tukaram's allegorical sequences of poems "in the manner of an adultress" and "Krishna and his playmates playing hide-and-seek using black blankets" are based on these aspects of Krishna lore.

Gopichandan:
white clay used in traditional medicine and also in rites and rituals in the form of a paste applied to parts of the body; the *Vaishnav Varkaris* of Maharashtra wear this as a mark of their cult, sect or faith especially on ceremonial occasions or during the rites of worship.

Govinda:
literally, "cow-finder" or "cow-gatherer"; another name for Krishna; like the name "Gopala", Tukaram uses this name too for Vitthal, making similar allegorical use of the lore of Krishna.

Hari:
another name for Vishnu, Hari literally means "fawn- coloured" and in this sense is perhaps synonymous with "Pandurang"; used as another name for Vitthal by Tukaram and other Marathi poet-saints; the various meanings of Hari in Sanskrit are: 1. green, greenish-yellow; tawny, bay, reddish-brown etc.; 2. it is a name not only for Vishnu but also for Indra, Shiva, Brahman, and Yama; it is connected with "*hara*" which means to take away, to remove, to relieve of, to seize, to captivate etc. and so may mean "the one who takes away", "the one who robs", "the one who relieves", "the one who seizes", "the one who attracts" etc.; thus it is a name that can be used in both positive and negative senses and therefore it has been applied to the protective Vishnu, the ascetic Shiva, to the conqueror Indra, and to Yama who takes away life, but this is only what one presumes.

Indrayani:
the river on whose banks Tukaram's village, Dehu, is situated; the same river also flows through the town of Alandi, sacred to all *Varkaris* because Jnanadev entered the state of *samadhi* there; the Indrayani at Dehu is associated with major events in Tukaram's

life as recorded in his poetry; the most important of these is the water-ordeal his notebooks were subjected to and the sequence of poems in which Tukaram poignantly describes his state of mind before and after their miraculous recovery after thirteen days; it is possible that his lyrical poems such as the one about "the pool of bliss" with its "ripples of bliss" and the one in which "water turns into sky" are transformations of actual images of the river by the side of which Tukaram might have spent much time reflecting on his experience of life.

Hero-stones:

"*viragala*" is the original Kannada word for these commemorative stones erected at the place of a warrior's or a saint's death to mark his martyrdom. Gunther D. Southeimer gives an illuminating account of these; since the image of Vitthal is strikingly unique in Hindu iconography, Deleury was prompted to observe that among the four other types of similar images are "the personages on the *viragalas* or hero-stones"; since the etymology of the name Vitthal is also contested, one of the suggestions put forward is that it is a compound word made by fusing "*vir*" (hero) and "*sthala*" (place).

Hrishikesha:

literally, "Lord of the senses", another name for Vishnu; also used for Vitthal by Tukaram; another name for Krishna; "*hrishika*" means an organ of sense and "*isha*" means Lord, God, master, or governor.

Jnanadev:

(1275–1296) one of the founders of the *Varkari* sect and also the first major poet in the Marathi language; he was also a philosopher and a saint; author of *Jnaneshwari, Anubhavamrita,* and several short poems; the first work is a long poetic discourse embodying a Marathi translation of the *Bhagawadgeeta* and the author's own commentary/interpretation; the second work is a long poem describing the descent of human awareness from a primordial cosmic being that produces the material world and all phenomena, and how an individual human being attains a state of oneness with the Cosmic Being by the grace of a g uru, becoming a liberated "self"; in poetry as well as in the *Varkari* sect, Tukaram is a lineal, spiritual descendant of Jnanadev; Namdeo, who initiated Tukaram

217

into poetry by appearing in his dream-like trance, was a spiritual disciple of Jnanadev, though Jnanadev was five years younger.

Jnaneshwari:

see Jnaneshwar or *Jnanadev* above; Jnanadev composed this work in 1290 when he was fifteen.

Kali-Yuga:

V.S. Apte's *Sanskrit-English Dictionary* defines Kali-Yuga as "the fourth age of the world, the iron age (consisting of 432,000 years of men and beginning from 8 February 3102 B.C.)"; however, "*Kali*" literally means dispute, dissension, quarrel, strife, contention; "*Yuga*" means "Age" or "Epoch"; in actual usage, mythical, epic, and poetic descriptions of *Kali-Yuga* are varied; it can be called the Age of Chaos, Age of Disorder, Age of Conflict, Age of Evil, Age of Sin, Age of Infidelity, Age of Dissipation, Age of Decadence, Age of Misrule, etc.; it is believed that the last *avatara* of Vishnu, Kalkin, will "descend to destroy the wickedness of this Age and liberate the world"; *Kali-Yuga* is our present Age, and it is the last and the worst of the Four Epochs; incidentally, "*kalka*" from which the name "Kalkin" derives, means grime, dirt, shit, filth, and also deceit, hypocrisy, meanness, wickedness, perversity, corruption, etc.; the thrust of the meaning is clear from this.

Karma:

"*karman*"; action or its consequences; seen in the context of the concept of reincarnation and the belief that a human being is liberated from the cycle of death and suffering only when the action and reaction produced by "*karma*" ceases, "*karma*" is a torturesome process of learning by trial and error, going through many births and deaths; Tukaram refers to the traditional belief that man has to pass through 840,000 experiences of birth, suffering, and death unless he sheds his bestial nature and sublimates himself; Tukaram believes, along with the tradition, that if a person's performance in the present life is faultless and fully meritorious, such a person will not have to be born again and go through the painful grind of transmigration; in Tukaram's view, *Bhakti* is the path of immediate salvation because the *Bhakta* spends his entire life in the worship of God; he is selfless and compassionate to all forms of life; he helps fellow human beings;

218

he is saintly and godlike in his kindness; the *Bhakta* is therefore
already liberated, in this very life, from the clutches of *karma*.

Kartika:
eighth lunar month of the Hindu calendar.

Kartiki:
the eleventh day of the bright half of the month of Kartika; see
Ekadashi above.

Kaustubha:
the legendary gem-stone or jewel obtained when the ocean was
churned by gods and demons for its secret gifts; the *Kaustubha* was
placed on Vishnu's breast; Tukaram describes Vitthal's image as
the image of Vishnu, and the *Kaustubha* comprises the pendant in
Vishnu's necklace in this image.

Keshava:
"long-haired" another name for Vishnu, used for Vitthal by
Tukaram.

Krishna:
"the dark one"; one of the three (Rama, Krishna, and the Buddha)
human *avataras* of Vishnu so far as "a son of man"; the divine
charioteer and guru of Arjuna who helped him recover his nerve
and overcome his self-conflict in the battlefield in the *Mahabharata*
war; divine author of the *Bhagawadgeeta*; earlier, the fun-loving
herdsman of Gokul and the lover of many milkmaids; the slayer of
wicked men and demons; the performer of many miracles;
Tukaram alludes to many of these contexts in his poems; for
Tukaram, Vitthal and Krishna are synonymous; therefore Vitthal's
wife, Rakhumai, is the same as Krishna's wife, Rukmini, and
Vishnu's wife, Lakshmi.

Mahar:
is one of low castes, in the Shudra category; in Maharashtra, the
Shudras were divided into different classes of village-servants
known as *balutedars*; these are distinct from government servants
and are sort of a servant sub-community entitled, for their services,
to be paid a fixed share of the agricultural produce; there are
twelve to eighteen kinds of *balutedars*, further subdivided into

classes or orders known as *kas* or *val*; the *mahars* belong to the first division; but in derogatory usage the word is similar to "nigger", "wog" and other racist or communal terms of contempt.

Maya:

literally,

1. a phantom image, an illusion, an apparition, a hallucination, an appearance, a dream, an unreality.

2. deceit, fraud, trick etc.

3. in Vedantic philosophy it is the mistaking of an ephemeral world for the Absoloute Being that is the true form of the immutable Supreme Spirit; in Samkhya philosophy, it is "nature" or the original source of the material world, consisting of the three elemental properties—*sattva*, *raja*, and *tama*;

4. compassion, pity, mercy, kindness; However, the word *"maya"* is related to the word *"ma"* which means, variously, "to measure", "to limit", "to compare", "to be in", "to find room in", "to be contained in": it can thus be related to "mother" and "womb" and by extension to "the world that contains us", "the space in which we are", "the dimensions that contain and confine us";

Tukaram is much more subtle and sophisticated than meets the eye because his sub-texts range from the *Bhagawadgeeta* to various philosophies current in India; he uses a simple, everyday language only occasionally using words like *"maya"* with their full charge of multiple significance. In one poem, he has used the colloquial Marathi word *"mav"* meaning *"maya"* in the sense of both "compassion" and "conjuror's trick", both "nature" and "the unreal world mistaken for Absolute Being": he deliberately uses the tensions between conflicting significance to create deliberate reversals of meaning or to produce, from one set of words, fully separated diverse images.

Moksha:

final liberation or salvation or emancipation from the cycle of *karma*, the wheel of death and suffering, or from a confined sense of self/individuality/ego; freedom from desire,attachment, memory, hope, anxiety, anguish and boredom which comprise the experience of this-worldly life.

Namdeo:

(1270-1350) one of the "Great Quartet" of "The Poets of Vithoba" (see *Jnanadev*, *Eknath*); one of the greatest poets in the Marathi language; author of a large body of lyrical, narrative, descriptive, autobiographical, didactic, incantatory, and ode-like *abhangs*; Namdeo had made an impulsive pledge, according to one of his own poems, that he would write one billion poems in praise of Vitthal, just like the monumental epic that Valmiki had written; Namdeo informs us that Vitthal himself tried to dissuade him from this unrealistic pledge pointing out that in the present age, human life was too short for a poet to be able to write one billion poems; in Tukaram's dream of initiation into poetry, Namdeo made a reference to this pledge and asked Tukaram to "write those I've left unwritten from the one billion I pledged"; there is gentle humour and irony in this aspect of an otherwise revelatory and solemn dream when we remember the context of Namdeo's original poem about his pledge and Vitthal's wry remark about the brevity of human life; a later poet, Niloba, who regarded Tukaram as his guru, thought that Tukaram was an *avatara* of Namdeo; indeed, there is a striking resemblance between some of the poetry of Namdeo and Tukaram, though Tukaram is distinguished by his horror of the human condition, personal anguish and will to transcend even *Bhakti* to achieve absolute enlightenment.

Name, the:

sometimes, this word has been treated as a proper noun because it refers specifically to one or more of the personal names by which the *Bhakta* knows, remembers, worships, and evokes his God; in the case of Tukaram this does not only refer to the name/s of Vitthal/Vishnu/ Krishna but also to the *mantra* (or device for meditative, inner recitation) given by Babaji, his guru: "*Rama Krishna Hari*", which again are names of Vishnu; the *Varkaris* sing, chant, or mentally recite by rote the various names of Vitthal/ Vishnu; "*Jai Jai Rama Krishna Hari*" has now become a slogan for them to raise at *bhajans* and *keertans*; most poet-saints have a sequence of poems that describe the power of "the Name"; each "name" is the evocation of a specific image of the deity since each name has its special aspect, allusion, association, mythical or legendary context; the poetry of proper nouns is inevitably lost in translation like the poetry of any culture-specific nouns—whether proper, common, personal, pronouns, or collective nouns; in folk, bardic and women's poetry this loss is crucial; Tukaram's poetry has roots in all three.

Narayana:

another name for Vishnu that means "son of man" or "son of the waters"; Tukaram uses this as another name for Vitthal; in the poems that refer to the ordeal-by-water to which Tukaram's notebooks were subjected, the radical, literal meaning assumes special significance; Vishnu or Narayana resides in the depths of a primordial ocean, stretched on his couch, the serpent of infinity; Narayana is thus one who resides in water; and it was from water that Tukaram's poems were returned undamaged after thirteen days.

Pandharpur:

Pandharpur lies to the south-east of Bombay, about 480 kilometers away, on the Deccan plateau; the river Bheema, which at this point is given the poetic name "Chandrabhaga" or "crescent moon", flows through the sacred city housing the premier shrine of Vitthal; it is an ancient settlement on a busy junction of old trade routes passing through a river valley; for the last seven hundred years *Varkari* pilgrims have been gathering here twice every year to attend the festival of Vitthal; the *Varkaris* believe that Vitthal is the form in which Vishnu himself landed on the Earth to visit his great devotee, Pundalik, and has been standing since on the "the Brick" on which Pundalik asked him "to wait for a while"; the cult of Vithoba or Vitthal is thus centred in Pandharpur as its sacred geographical nucleus; a Maharashtra-wide network of pilgrim-routes meets at this centre; Pandharpur is also the city where the poet-saints and devotees of Vithoba gave a shape to the Marathi language and its literary culture by assimilating the dialects of various pilgrims and disseminated a sense of equality, brother-hood, and spiritual community; Tukaram has several poems about Pandharpur and its sacred importance; he also addresses Vitthal quite often as the "Lord of Pandharpur"; Tukaram has stressed the importance of the pilgrimage and the *Varkari* way of life; but it is not clear whether Tukaram regularly visited Pandharpur himself; he has an epistolatory poem to Vitthal "sent" with *Varkari* pilgrims; in another poem he describes himself as waiting anxiously for news from Pandharpur and news about Vitthal's welfare; *Varkaris* symbolically carry the "spirit of Tukaram" from Dehu to

Pandharpur on their regular pilgrimage; this custom is followed till this day; all their beloved saints from Jnanadev to Tukaram are believed to be present in spirit at every festival in Pandharpur; traditions of the poetry of the saints are maintained in an oral form and as performed songs through the living medium of the pilgrimage and the festival in which it culminates.

Pandurang:

another name for Vitthal, used for the first time in the thirteenth century according to Deleury.

Pundalik:

also "Pundarika" and "Paundarika". See "*Brick, the*".

Puranas:

medieval compilations of myths concerning various deities of the Hindu pantheon; they are regarded as part of the scriptures.

Rebirth:

also "reincarnation"; traditional Hindu belief that man is successively born and dies until his individual spiritual evolution is complete; see *karma*.

Rukmini:

Krishna's principal wife; Tukaram considers her synonymous with Vitthal's wife, Rakhuma, also referring to her as Rakhumai (Mother Rakhuma), Rakhumadevi (Goddess Rakhuma), Rakhumabai (Lady Rakhuma) etc., Vitthal-Rakhuma, Krishna-Rukmini, and Lakshmi-Vishnu are synonymous couples and are often iconographically shown together or close to each other.

Santaji Teli Jagnade:

a devoted companion of Tukaram; his notebooks contain the only contemporary copies of some of Tukaram's work.

Tukaram:

"Tuka" is the dimunitive as well as abbreviated form of the full name "Tukaram"; Tukaram's family name is "Moré", a Maratha clan-name; his father's name was Bolhoba and mother's Kanakai; Tukaram describes himself as a Shudra *kunbi* or a non-caste peasant.

The name Tukaram is somewhat obscure; there is a goddess named Tukai, sometimes the name is used for the Goddess Amba at Tuljapur in Maharashtra; it is clear that this word is "*Tuka* plus *aai*" and "*aai*" means mother in Marathi; but Tuka remains unexplained; however, there is the Marathi noun "*tuk*" which means importance; weighing; measuring; sizing up; balancing; weighing in a balance; the verb "*tukane*" has similar meanings; it also means to be equal to something in weight, size, or importance and also to appreciate, to assess, to evaluate; or to balance, equalize, to make symmetrical, to make poised, to counterbalance; and it also means to reflect, to consider, to reconcile, to square up; finally, it means to nod, to give assent to, to acquiesce etc. "Rama" of course is the name of an *avatara* of Vishnu. Tukaram has used the abstract noun "*tuk*" as well as the verb "*tukane*" in various places in the proximity of his signature-line, "Says Tuka"; one line goes as follows: "*Tuka tuki tukala*"; there are several puns in these three words; *Tuka*, the proper noun, is the subject, followed by the locative form of the same noun used as the object, and lastly the verb "*tukane*" used in the simple past tense, third person singular; read in the context of the above meanings, the line becomes a translator's nightmare.

Tulsi:

the sweet basil or the black basil, a plant sacred to Vitthal and to Vishnu; all *Vaishnavs* (devotees of Vishnu or children of Vishnu) worship the plant itself; it is grown in the courtyard of their houses in a little squarish-shaped clay-tower or pot called *vrindavan*; Vitthal and Vishnu both are supposed to wear a necklace or a rosary-like garland of *tulsi*-wood beads; the images of Vitthal and Vishnu are offered *tulsi*-leaves during the performance of rites of worship; a *Varkari* wears a *tulsi*-bead necklace or rosary when he takes his initial vow; and whenever he goes on a pilgrimage to Pandharpur he wears it; some of them wear it all the time.

Varkari:

is one who makes a "*vari*", which in Marathi means, "round trip" or "pilgrimage" or "regular visit to a place and return from it"; a *Varkari* is vowed and committed to undertake, twice every year, a pilgrimage to Pandharpur to attend the Ashadhi and the Kartiki festivals of Vitthal; this is scrupulously observed by every *Varkari;* *Varkaris* also avoid eating meat, refrain from intoxicants and stimulants, and follow certain other regulations and codes of conduct; see also, *Ashadhi, Kartiki, Vitthal, Dehu, Alandi, Pandhar-pur*, etc.

Vedas :

the four earliest Hindu scriptures; Rigveda, Yajurveda, Samaveda, and Atharvaveda; the fourth Veda is a later addition and the first three are still known as "the sacred triad"; they are believed to have been the self-revelation of the Absolute/Supreme/Whole Being or *Brahman* Itself, and therefore not man-made; for this reason they are also known as *shrutis* or "revealed and heard sound" as distinct from the man-made compositions of sages that are known as *smritis* or "recollections"; "revelations" and "recol-lections" could be a short way of naming them; Tukaram often alludes to the Vedas and he seems to have had a sophisticated acquaintance with them though he points, often with mock-humility, to his non-caste status and "ignorance"; Tukaram's Brah-min detractors, according to his own account as well as Bahinabai's autobiography, considered him an ignorant upstart because as a Shudra, access to the Vedas was forbidden to him; when he sheds his feigned self-derogation, Tukaram talks equally confidently of knowing the secret teachings of the Vedas; Tukaram perceives his own poetry as "revealed by God"; he says, "God speaks through me"; he goes to the extent of denying all credit for authorship, owning only ignorance and lack of eloquence as his personal flaws but asserting that the truth he is expressing is "not man-made" but "divine"; this is exactly the claim that is made on behalf of the "revelations" of the *shrutis*; to Tukaram, all genuine poetry is revelatory as much as the *shrutis* are; this gives us two fundamental categories of poetry, like the two applied to the scriptures them-selves: "revealed poetry" and "recollected poetry"; if the Vedas are poetry, Tukaram's poetry is often Veda-like; if religion itself is poetry like the Vedas, Tukaram's poetry is religion; Tukaram's non-dualism is so radical that he makes no difference between poetry and religion, perceiving both as revelations of Absolute Being; his mysticism itself is a radical, revolutionary stance; this is the poetics of Tukaram's spirituality; when Tukaram says, "We alone know the meaning of the Vedas", he is saying that both poetry and the Vedas are revealed language or recollected language pointing to a vast non-discursive truth: their validity lies in what they are pointing to: like painted arrows, they only signify and direct attention.

Vishnu:

"the pervader"; originally a solar god, then the supreme god, for which position he vies with Shiva; see *Vitthal, Ananta, Narayana, Govinda, Gopala, Hrishikesha, Keshava, Rama, Krishna, Hari,* etc.—all these are synonymous in Tukaram's poetry with God, Lord, Master, Maker, Creator, *Brahman,* Absolute Being, Whole Being, Primordial Being, Being, Bliss, Beatitude, etc. each specific name, however, signifies a specific aspect or perception of "the One" or the "all-inclusive Being"; Tukaram is a *Vaishnava* monotheist but as an enlightened mystic, his monotheism transcends names.

Vitthal:

also, in Tukaram, Vithoba (Father Vitthal), Vithu (Vitthal addressed with the familiarity of a close friend), Vithabai ("Lady Vitthal" a feminized form of the masculine noun; Tukaram sometimes drops the formality and uses the word in the sense of Mother). The origin of the name Vitthal is obscure, uncertain, and contested; one is not sure when this name was used first but, like Pandurang, it seems to have emerged into literary usage some time in the thirteenth century.

The native "region" of the name Vitthal radiates from Pandharpur throughout Maharashtra, parts of Karnataka, and parts of Andhra Pradesh which were often one large political unit in the history of the Deccan; the name Vitthal does not seem to have any roots in Sanskrit and it could be of Dravidian origin; in Jnanadev's time, when the name Vitthal started gaining wide currency, Marathi vocabulary already had a significant content of Kannada and Telugu and some distinct traces of Tamil, so this may not be as far-fetched as it seems.

The iconography of Vitthal is unique and intriguing; the best way to begin to approach it is by trying to describe the image and its stance, treating the Pandharpur image as central.

In brief, Vitthal's image at Pandharpur is a male figure, stone-black in colour, and standing erect on a raised slab known as "the Brick"; arms akimbo and hands on hips, the figure is perfectly symmetrical; in terms of proportions, it is a stocky figure of medium build; the feet are placed evenly together, as though standing to attention, and the eyes seem to be looking straight ahead; the crown is cylindrical though in some images it is also conical; there are fish-shaped rings in both the ears; the image is adorned with sweet basil beads turned into a necklace; the left hand holds a sea-conch and the right hand holds the stalk of a lotus though in some images it makes the gesture of blessing as traditionally understood; the cloth that covers the loins is skin-tight and the shape of the genitals shows through the garment; sometimes, Vitthal's image is accompanied by the image of his wife, Rakhuma.

The image and the stance of Vitthal have been read in many different ways that amplify or go beyond the actual visual appearance.

Scholars contest both the image and the name of Vitthal, offering diverse hypotheses about their origin; briefly, Vitthal has been connected variously with Vishnu, or a cattle-god, or a hero-stone, and even with the Buddha; the worshippers of Vitthal have seen him, for the last seven hundred years, only as a form of Vishnu.

The poetic "iconography" of Vitthal, or Vitthal as described by poets in their own words since Jnanadev and Namdeo, follows a core of conventions and joint-stock phraseology, though each poet has added his own unique flourishes to the description.

Tukaram's poem describing the image and the stance of Vitthal, apparently simple and elegant, contains an enigmatic element that may crucially influence one's reading; he begins the poem literally with the following three words: "*sundar te dhyana*" or in the same literal order and word-for-word "beautiful that..." the third word is the enigmatic one; while "beautiful" can be rendered with a choice of synonyms with some family-resemblance among them, "*dhyana*"—the third word—can mean "(that) character" in a colloquial sense, or "(that) meditating (figure)" which are very diverse in their meaning; the word is a forked sign; Tukaram refers to the mythology of Vishnu by pointing to the "*Kaustubha*", a fabulous gem-stone obtained when the gods and the demons churned the ocean to receive its legendary secret gifts; this gem-stone was placed on the breast of Vishnu; the fish-shaped or crocodile-shaped earrings also belong to the mythological description of Vishnu; the conch-shell and the tulsi-bead necklace are of course obvious and not imagined or finely perceived; Tukaram is not merely a worshipper of Vishnu; he has a mythopoetic imagination, the need to create a legend to satisfy in the process of worship; he also has an emotional need to find the exact words; and finally, he has the urge to explore the many sub-texts in which a literary or poetic image of Vishnu is rooted; he has to be faithful to the physical precision of the sculptured image that is so well-known and seen by almost his entire audience; yet he also has to grace it with poetic creativity.

MORE ABOUT PENGUINS

For further information about books available from Penguins in India write to Penguin Books (India) Ltd, B4/246, Safdarjung Enclave, New Delhi 110 029.

In the UK: For a complete list of books available from Penguins in the United Kingdom write to Dept. EP, Penguin Books Ltd, Harmondsworth, Middlesex UB7 0DA.

In the U.S.A.: For a complete list of books available from Penguins in the United States write to Dept. DG, Penguin Books, 299 Murray Hill Parkway, East Rutherford, New Jersey 07073.

In Canada: For a complete list of books available from Penguins in Canada write to Penguin Books Canada Ltd, 2801 John Street, Markham, Ontario L3R 1B4.

In Australia: For a complete list of books available from Penguins in Australia write to the Marketing Department, Penguin Books Australia Ltd, P.O. Box 257, Ringwood, Victoria 3134.

In New Zealand: For a complete list of books available from Penguins in New Zealand write to the Marketing Department, Penguin Books (N.Z.) Ltd, Private Bag, Takapuna, Auckland 9.